TOM GREEN

TOM GREEN

UDDER INSANITY

SHANNON HAWKINS

ECW Press

The publication of *Tom Green* has been generously supported by
the Canada Council, the Ontario Arts Council, and
the Government of Canada through the
Book Publishing Industry Development Program.

CANADIAN CATALOGUING IN PUBLICATION DATA
Hawkins, Shannon
Tom Green: udder insanity
ISBN 1-55022-406-9
1. Green, Tom. 2. Comedians – Canada – Biography. I. Title.
PN2308.G73H38 2000 791.45'028'092 C00-930433-9

Cover design by Guylaine Régimbald.
Front cover photo by Ken Kerr/*Toronto Sun*.
Back cover photo by Fred Chartrand.
Interior design by Yolande Martel.

Printed by Printcrafters Inc., Winnipeg, Manitoba, Canada.
Distributed in Canada by General Distribution Services,
325 Humber College Blvd., Etobicoke, Ontario M9W 7C3.
Distributed in the United States by LPC Group,
1436 West Randolph Street, Chicago, Illinois, U.S.A. 60607.
Distributed in Europe by Turnaround Publisher Services,
Unit 3, Olympia Trading Estate,
Coburg Road, Wood Green, London N2Z 6TZ.

Published by ECW PRESS,
2120 Queen Street East, Suite 200,
Toronto, Ontario M4E 1E2.
www.ecw.ca/press

PRINTED AND BOUND IN CANADA

*To my love, Lee Michael,
for your unwavering support*

TABLE OF CONTENTS

ACKNOWLEDGMENTS

Writing this book has allowed me the opportunity to achieve some of my own journalistic aspirations, which would have not been possible without the help of some very generous people in my life. First and foremost I would like to pay special tribute to a good friend, Kimberly Bain. Through her wisdom and expertise, she has given me guidance and offered extremely valuable suggestions for each chapter.

As with most untold stories this could not have been seen to fruition without those people willing to share their most personal memories. Tom Green's animated personality has touched the lives of some very special people, who have in turn nurtured him and shared their recollections of these encounters: Mike Bullard, Sean and Elaine Dickinson, Hugh and Greg Campbell, Ed Robinson, Scott Henderson, Ken Rockburn, Kerry MacLean, Shirley Gaudreau, Ivan Berry, Darcy De Toni, Trevor Cavanagh, Ian Thorn, Ian Lewer, Howard Wagman, Tom Stewart, Johnny Vegas, Karen McHarg, Chris Mullington, Allan Pressman, Slawko Klymkiw, Mickey Stackpole, Dean Foster, Don Cuddy, Gisele Wewer, Dez Fitzgerald, Steve Jarosz, Susan Terrill, and Jon Harris. Without their candid interviews this book would not have been possible.

Thank you to Merilyn Read and Danielle Lacelle of MTR Entertainment for their candor and compassion in talking with me about the good old days of producing *The Tom Green Show* out of the Arts Court Theater. Ray Skaff, Marlene Murray, Karen Pickles, and the crew at Rogers Community TV were a blessing in their help with digging up archived footage of the show. They were gracious enough to allow me hours and hours of time in their editing suites to watch footage, from the very first episode to the last one taped at Rogers studio. Tom has become a success story for the community station and their pride in his achievements is evident.

Thanks as well to Rogers, MTR Entertainment, The Comedy Network, and Pepsi One for supplying video footage.

I would like also to express my gratitude to ECW Press for granting me the opportunity to take on this project, particularly Robert Lecker, Holly Potter, Jennifer Lokash, and Megan Ferrier for their wisdom, and most importantly Alana Wilcox for editing this book with a sense of humor.

Above all I could not have penned this story without the support of some very special friends and colleagues who have encouraged me to accept new roles with fervor and explore every avenue with creativity and zest: Rick and Maureen VanSickle; Mark Bonokoski; Vince and Gail Bain; Tracy Elliott; Doug, Celeste, Megan, and Sean Walker; Drew McAnulty; Paula Jackson; Calvin James; Wendy Daniels; Tony Caldwell; Tara Hatoum; Christine, Mike, Cynthia, and Samantha Feagan; Mike Therien; Diane Langdon; Mitch and Gloria Axelrad; Jillienne, Pat, and Rinaldo; Kim Rohac; Andrea Fleck; Holly Mayhew; and Emily Reid. And I extend a heartfelt thank-you most of all to my loving family, whose encouragement and guidance have given me the confidence to complete this biography. Mom, Dad, Kelly, Erin, Tara, Rob, Christopher, Grandma, Grandpa, Jason, and Henley, and the entire Hawkins, Mehlenbacher, Piro, and Hogan clans — you are all truly my inspiration.

Shannon Hawkins, Ottawa, Ontario

PREFACE

Who ever would have thought that watching a grown man stuff a wriggling handful of live earthworms in his mouth would be considered entertainment? That seems like a rhetorical question, but there's an answer — comedian and talk-show host Tom Green. Whether he's happily munching on a mushed-up ball of Vaseline and human hair or turning his parents' bungalow into a petting zoo, Tom manages to astonish viewers with every glimpse into his demented mind. He combines a childlike naivete, a teenage curiosity, and a decidedly adult intelligence into a wacky sense of humor that continually delights and bewilders his ever-growing audience. Every week Tom Green invites his fans to temporarily duck out of their lives of responsibility and maturity and, for even a little while, look at the world through Green-colored glasses.

I'll never forget the first time I entered the bizarre world of Tom Green. I had been contacted by his producer, Merilyn Read of Ottawa-based MTR Entertainment, to interview the rising star in the summer of 1998 while he was back in Ottawa on a break from filming the movie *Superstar*. I can laugh now, but I must confess that before I met the star of the notorious *Tom Green Show* for the first time I was afraid, petrified even — not of Green himself per se, but rather of what he might do. The host of *The Tom Green Show* had a reputation around town for being a loose cannon.

As I arrived at MTR's offices, I felt nervous. I sat in my car in the parking lot, checking my watch repeatedly and loading and reloading the

tape in my recorder. After years of watching Green's show on Rogers
Community TV and The Comedy Network, my imagination got the better of me. I'd had dreams the night before of roadkill raccoons and plaid
houses. I envisioned him dressed in full scuba gear — complete with
face mask, flippers, wet suit, and oxygen tank — holding a can of
whipped cream. During the interview he'd run around the studio and
every time I got up enough courage to ask him a question he'd retaliate
by launching the cream at me. Like anyone who's seen the show, I knew
that I couldn't even begin to imagine what kind of crazy prank Tom had
in store for me. I was certain he would arrive armed with a camcorder
to videotape the entire interview — including my extreme humiliation,
whatever it might be — to use later that season as a segment on the
show.

Swallowing my fear, I walked into the building and introduced myself
to the receptionist. I was shown into one of the editing suites at General
Assembly Production Center, and I anxiously peered around the room.
A bank of ominous-looking computers stared at me from one side, an
imposing bureau from the other. Taking a deep breath, I walked over
and sat down in one of the black swivel chairs hidden behind the desk.
I couldn't help but think, more than once, that I should for my own sanity have offered to conduct the interview over the phone. But my curiosity had gotten the better of me. I wanted to meet the ingenious man
who had managed to so completely captivate his young audience — and
dispel the unfounded rumor that everyone from Ottawa is staunchly
conservative and possesses the spontaneity of a wet sponge. A knock
on the door interrupted my thoughts. "Hi, I'm Tom Green. You must be
Shannon," said the solemn-faced intruder. He extended a hand in my
direction and in sheer terror I grasped it with a grip even Mike Tyson
would be proud of. "Sorry, I'm a little late. Have you been waiting long?"
he asked.

Waiting long? He actually sounded concerned. Who was this guy and
why was he masquerading as the remorseless Tom Green? He didn't look
the part at all. There was no whipped cream. There was no scuba suit
and nary a flipper in sight. This young man had an armful of videotapes
and a pile of file folders crammed full of papers. "Sorry," he repeated.
"I'm just swamped with editing and work for the show 'cause we just

got back from our cross-Canada road trip." He plunked himself down in a chair opposite me and began describing some of the deadlines he had coming up in the near future.

So this really *was* Tom Green. How bizarre, I thought, that the man who appeals to so many viewers because of his utter disregard for authority and the laws of nature would parade around as a hardworking, young go-getter, eager to take on challenges and prove himself to the world. He spoke animatedly about his road trip and his recent role in the big-screen flick *Superstar*. "Things are getting really busy and hectic," he said, pointing to piles of tapes. "I'm sort of in a quiet mode right now, recharging my batteries." He went on to describe the method behind his madness, beginning with how he goes into character for the show-biz bits. "When I'm out performing I go into a different character or different zone," he explained. Then, as if he could read my mind, he continued. "As you can see, I'm not covering myself in whipped cream right now." On the contrary, he was quite reserved. He was eager to talk about the inner workings of his show, but kept his feelings about his career to himself.

So if this Tom Green wasn't the oddball comic that we see on TV, then where does Tom end and the Greening begin? As most people in the industry will attest, Tom Green, the person, is a self-motivated individual who has been working diligently to reach the spotlight for years. As for those who have been targets of his goofy irreverence, well, they might have another story. Just the same, Tom Green has single-handedly managed to freshen up the face of TV comedy for younger audiences. He is, to say the least, an intriguing figure for investigation. There is more to him than the outrageous persona he presents to the public. Where did he come from and how did he get where he is? What makes him tick and how does he muster up the courage to make fun of complete strangers on the street and embarrass his loving parents?

Buckle up your seatbelt — the story of the Greening of North America is about to begin. . . .

INTRODUCTION

Flopping himself down into one of the oversized chairs in the aptly named Green Room at the MTV studios in New York City, Tom was visibly exhausted. After his countless hours in the editing suite with producers and in meetings with writers, the first three shows were finished and ready for audience approval by the last week in January 1999. The long, grueling hours had taken their toll on the host. His deep-set eyes looked bleary in the low lighting and his tall frame seemed skinnier than ever.

"Do you think I look too thin?" he asked in a comical tone. "People have been saying I'm looking a little like Ally McBeal," he said, holding up one of his wrists for inspection. "What do you think?" The remark was so matter-of-fact and out of the blue that the handful of other people sitting in the room couldn't help but laugh. "What's so funny?" he demanded of the crowd. Even without a camera present it was apparent Tom was still in character, his mind constantly at work to find ways to make people laugh. Collecting himself from the chair he side-stepped his way towards the door. His long legs started to move as soon as he stepped out into the hallway. A funky hip-hop beat was coming from the swell of mtv workers standing just outside the door. "Oh, yeaaaaah!" he cried out. Within seconds his entire body responded to the beat and Tom gyrated into the sea of faces. All that remained of the host was his emphatic voice as it echoed down the long corridor. "I am not skinnnnnny, I'm not skinnnnnny."

For Tom, being the center of attention is nothing new. Since the first grade he's made a point of getting himself noticed. Parents, teachers, and fellow students — he used them all as guinea pigs while honing his skills as a comedian. Tom has always been successful at pushing people to their limits by catching them off guard and sucking them into his own world. The first time Tom walked onstage at his high school students' council assembly and whipped up a tossed salad as part of his speech, his classmates knew they were witnessing history in the making. He tried everything — radio, stand-up, and music — but it wasn't until he tried his hand at television broadcasting that he found his true love.

From the moment *The Tom Green Show* went on the air, it attracted a cult-like following among its viewers. As the show grew and developed its niche on the Rogers Community station in Ottawa, then The Comedy Network across Canada, and eventually the massive MTV Network, his audience has followed every step. Fans adore the stars, Tom, Derek, Glenn, and Phil, and all their crazy stunts. Hundreds of different websites have popped up on the Internet, with the flagship www.tomgreen.com receiving thousands of hits a week. Due to the no-holds-barred manner of the host and the anything-goes format of the program, viewers knew they were witnessing a special type of show right from the start. It was a refreshing change from what conventional broadcasters were offering, and fans latched on to *The Tom Green Show*. The response has been phenomenal from around the globe. "Why don't you come film some stuff here," writes one fan from Australia. "It would be great if you could come over to my house and build a real igloo," suggests another from Alaska. Who knows — maybe one day Tom just might do that.

The support for Tom, Glenn, Derek, and Phil has been tremendous. Fans on the official Tom Green website have written professing their undying love. "This is the funniest show I've ever seen. I love you for the pains you bring to my sides when I watch the show. I think that my neighbors think I am crazy," e-mails one adoring fan from South Carolina. "I think it is so cool the way you keep a straight face throughout your skits," writes another from New South Wales. For others Tom has become somewhat of an atypical sex symbol. "Tom, I just wanna say that you are one hot babe," gushes a fan from Connecticut. "Tom Green rules," writes another fan from New Jersey. "His show is the funniest ever created and I give credit to him for having the guts to do what he does. I'm in love with him."

Bizarre is the only way to describe some of the comments popping up in the chat rooms. They range from viewers pleading for Tom to appear at their school to off-the-wall personal questions. "I am graduating from college this weekend and as tradition would have it, I need to pull off a student prank," explains a fan from Minnesota. "Any ideas . . . something legal?" Another writes, "I'm having trouble naming my new cat, any suggestions?"

Some of Tom's fans have even dreamed of becoming the next Tom Green, e-mailing in descriptions of the different stunts they've pulled off in their hometowns. "Me and my friends in Victoria are huge fans of yours, mainly because we want to be like you. I walked down the street with a bike tire and ketchup on my shirt and then I fell down and someone stopped and talked to me. We taped it too!" a fan from British Columbia writes. "Then I put a cardboard box over my head that had 'Jesus' written on it and ran down the street chasing cars." Other fans have logged-on to the *Tom Green Show* website to offer suggestions for pranks they've always wanted Tom to pull. "You should get a cardboard box and paint it so it looks like a car," explains an Ontario fan. "Then you run out and make noises like you are a real car and act as if you break down." Another fan from Louisiana suggests that Tom act like the nonsmoking police. "I think Tom needs to walk around the street with a fire extinguisher, threatening people who light up a cigarette."

The result of his success is that many of his fans have tried to live vicariously through Tom's deranged sense of humor. "Tom, it is hilarious when you prank your parents," says one wanna-be from Pennsylvania. "Really it's what all of us dream and fantasize about doing but just don't have the guts to do." Some hard-core fans still adore their radical hero while feeling pangs of sympathy for his poor parents. "*The Tom Green Show* is so outrageous and funny . . . it's so cool, but the one thing that is too wacked out is when Tom's parents are involved. His poor parents," empathizes one Washington fan. "How inconsiderate. It's hilarious if he bugs people who he doesn't even know, but not his poor parents."

Having relocated to New York City, and eventually to Los Angeles, Tom is safely out of the Ottawa area code, and his loving parents, Richard and Mary Jane, can breathe a little bit easier. Perhaps they'll have a bit of a reprieve from the constant presence of Tom's video cameras invading their lives. What most viewers don't know is that those stunts where Tom tries to embarrass his parents on national television were sparked by an incident in his childhood. "I had to get them back for the hell they put me through," he said melodramatically, recalling his life as a rambunctious kid. "Every summer they would wake me up at 7 a.m. before they went to work because I didn't have a summer job."

The outcome of those hellish teenage years was that Tom went from freeloading son to rap star and finally to comic genius on MTV's *The Tom Green Show*. Along the way he has mocked everything conventional broadcasting stands for. He's allowed himself very few limitations; he has done everything from sucking a cow's udder to microwaving a dead raccoon. It's his job to embarrass innocent bystanders by incorporating them into his world of chaotic humor. No one is safe from Tom's probing camera lens. He lurks in the shadows of the absurd, waiting to pounce on the unsuspecting. Where does his inspiration come from? You are about to find out. Welcome to the slightly askew world of Tom Green.

1

RUDE AWAKENINGS

As he tiptoed in through the back door of his parents' house, it took a moment for Tom's eyes to adjust to the darkness. Navigating a path around the kitchen furniture, he made his way soundlessly into the living room, and, stopping midstride, peered into the darkness for signs of life. Glancing down the first-floor corridor that led to his parents' bedroom, he breathed a sigh of relief as nobody stirred. Everyone was still sound asleep. He'd managed to sneak in past curfew again after another summer evening of kamikaze skateboarding with his friends. Taking off his sneakers and leaving them on the living room floor, he quietly descended the back stairs to deposit his skateboard in the rec room. "One, two, three, four," he said to himself, mentally calculating how many hours' sleep he could get in before his parents got up for work. "That's plenty of time." Sneaking into his disheveled bedroom he switched on the small lamp in the corner. He stumbled through the piles of clothes, skateboarding stuff, and music equipment littering the floor and flopped limply down on the bed. Rolling over, he grabbed his clock from the bedside table and set the alarm for 6 a.m. He pulled the comforter up over his body and drifted off to sleep.

It felt like only a few moments before 6 a.m. arrived. On cue, the blaring alarm clock signaled the dawn of a new day. Tom silenced the annoying ring with a smack. A moment later he bolted upright and stared at the ceiling, listening intently for footsteps from overhead. Silence. Absolute silence. Throwing the covers on the floor, Tom grabbed a pillow from the bed and a T-shirt from the pile of laundry scattered on the floor and then rushed for the basement stairs, trying to make as little noise as possible and looking over his shoulder to make sure no one was watching him. Satisfied he was alone, Tom pushed aside the retractable door hiding the opening under the stairs. He stuffed himself into the damp crawl space and closed the door softly behind him. Alone in the tiny quarters, he nestled his head down into the pillow and drifted off to sleep with a goofy, self-satisfied smile on his face. His parents would never find him there. He was safe for another day from their threat of forced summer employment. He would make it his full-time job to spend the summer outsmarting them and avoiding doing any real labor. There was no way he was going to spend his teen years working at some mind-numbing job. He had bigger plans and his parents were just going to have to accept it, or else try to find him. Either way it was more exciting than scouring the want ads.

"I just wanted to spend my summer skateboarding and they were really kind of strict about, like, getting jobs," Tom said, recalling his childhood during one interview. "They really wanted me to work." Tom's parents had bigger career goals for their eldest son. They weren't too keen on his plans to spend the summer lounging around their Beacon Hill home or wasting his days skateboarding. As soon as June rolled around, Richard and Mary Jane began their ritual pleas for Tom to get a job. "Every summer they'd wake me up every morning at 7 a.m.," said Tom, thinking back to those mornings as a 15-year-old kid trying to outsmart his parents. "And I'd been out skateboarding till 3 a.m. the night before. It was crazy. The scenes in the morning were crazy when I was a kid."

When the Greens finally realized their pleas for Tom to obtain gainful employment were being ignored, they decided to try a new approach. If reasoning with him wasn't going to work, they'd have to retaliate at his own level. Before the pair left for the office they'd creep into Tom's bedroom and hover over his sleeping body, waiting for just the right moment to strike. One would stand at the foot of the bed, ready to yank the covers off the sleeping lump, while the other would be poised at the center ready with a jug of water. In one quick motion the covers would go flying across the room and Tom would jump from the bed just as the cold liquid splashed against his bare stomach. Howling with the agony of a wounded seal, Tom, now cold and soaking wet, vowed to get even with his parents. This meant war! In fact, it only took a few early morning wake-ups before he devised a plan of his own. There was no way he was going to let them have the upper hand. He started eluding them by finding strategic places around the house where he could hide from their disruptions to his beauty sleep. He'd make little sleeping areas behind the furnace or under the basement stairs, then set his alarm for 6 a.m., when he'd sneak into his makeshift bed and fall back to sleep until he heard his parents leave for work. "That's eventually what I had to resort to doing," Tom laughed. "Then I'd go back to my bed and sleep until noon."

The cat-and-mouse games, both Tom and his parents have confessed, lasted for most of Tom's teen years. The stunts changed daily, as did the score. On occasions when Tom was the victor, he'd claim he "broke them in 'cause they finally realized they weren't going to get me to work that way." Those times when his parents came out on top he'd end up skateboarding down the streets of Ottawa searching for summer employment. "I did get jobs," he confessed. "I did always end up working at some crazy construction job 'cause my dad would make me go find a job in construction."

Knowing that from an early age Tom had a mind and personality of his own, Richard Green was constantly trying to convince him to learn a trade. "So I'd spend the whole summer knocking asbestos out of ceilings," Tom said, chuckling to himself. "He was in the military and he wanted me to do something like working in a carpentry shop carving wood." But hammering nails or fixing a leaky kitchen faucet wasn't exactly what Tom had in mind. If he was going to get a job, it was going to have to be something creative and entertaining. The answer came with a simple phone call — telemarketing, of course. Contracted by an Ottawa company, Tom said he spent the summer days doing telephone sales. Well, sort of. "I always ended up working in telemarketing 'cause I'd get to do crank calls all day," Tom said. What actually happened, without anyone even knowing it, was that Tom was using his job experiences as a training ground for his comedy. He was developing some very crafty schemes, especially where his parents were concerned — an invaluable skill in his future career.

*

On the surface Richard and Mary Jane Green seem like your typical, ordinary parental figures. Richard, a retired military captain, and Mary Jane, a communications consultant, both worked hard and tried to instill a sense of values and rules in their children. Both Tom and his younger brother, Joe, grew up with a good moral background. "We tried for a strict household, but Tom's not good at rules," said Richard Green. "I think he eventually won 'cause we gave up."

Even as a child, Tom was always a little bit of a hell-raiser, a noticeable contrast to his younger brother's shy and quiet demeanor. His parents had a hard time trying to keep up with Tom's boisterous personality. "He was a rambunctious kid, always very talkative, very active, and he never sat still," Mary Jane said while flipping through a stack of old photographs in the living room of their Gloucester home. She couldn't help but laugh as she picked up a photograph of Tom at age five. "I always said he looked like Alfred E. Neuman from *MAD* magazine," she said, chuckling at the old photo of her eldest son in a brown plaid poly-ester pantsuit. While their memories of Tom remain fond, over the years they have definitely had their share of trouble keeping him in line. It seems he was never one to conform to the rules; he simply made up his own and cajoled others into following his lead.

Tom was born on July 30, 1971, in Pembroke, Ontario, and the Greens soon followed Richard's military career to Canada's capital. Tom's mis-chievous childhood was spent in Beacon Hill, a community exploding in size in the '80s as families with university backgrounds and govern-ment or military employment flocked to the Orleans area, only a few minutes' drive from Ottawa. It was a fairly sophisticated neighborhood that Tom spent his youth disrupting; with military and diplomatic ties, the families often traveled a lot, bringing up their children with a solid foundation of worldly knowledge before they even ventured off to school.

Like the other Beacon Hill offspring, Tom entered the hallowed halls of Robert Hopkins Public School for his elementary years and Henry Munro Middle School for grades seven and eight. Both schools count Hollywood heartthrob Tom Cruise and Canadian rocker Bryan Adams

among their alumni. Robert Hopkins was modeled after the British
"open-concept" style. With only three main classrooms, the student body
was separated into groups A (kindergarten, grades one and two), B (three
and four), and C (five and six), with the only division between them
being the cumbersome blackboards the teachers used to try to cordon
off their areas. "We could create these quasi-classrooms," said Tom's
sixth-grade teacher, Shirley Gaudreau. "But the sound always traveled."
It was during these early years that Tom got his first real audience as a
comedian.

The school's open-concept design gave the students freedom to
express their talents and creativity. In Shirley's classroom that sense of
independence ran rampant, and it was there that Tom Green started his
career. From early on in the year she was a witness to Tom's budding
sense of humor. "Tommy was always hyper, he had a lot of energy," she
recalled as she sorted through some of her old class photographs.
"Children who are talented creatively, they learn differently. They talk and
act differently." Because of the classroom design, the moment Tom
would start goofing around, his friends' laughter would draw crowds
from other classes in the vicinity. Shirley recalled frequently having to
call out, "Oh Tommy, sit down!" or "Children, quiet please."

A born Canadian! Tom plays for the North Gloucester Stars (1985–86)
(back row, second player from the left)
COURTESY SHANNON HAWKINS

But it wasn't his humor that gave Shirley her impression of him as someone who had exceptional talents. It was after a Morrison-McCall standardized test for literature that she recognized his abilities. Tom scored among the top percentile in his grade six class, testing at a grade eight level. "He was smart and it really showed in his quick repartee. He was a very active kid. We sometimes had to peel him off the walls," she said. In fact he was into everything from artwork to science projects — so much so that she usually found herself running nonstop until the bell rang to signal the end of the school day. "I could never sit down in class and say, 'Let's have quiet time now,'" she said.

That was until February of 1983. It was during an annual class project that she realized how she could get a break from Tom's constant energy and enthusiasm. Traditionally Mrs. Gaudreau had each student perform for their classmates a three- to five-minute speech on a topic of their choice. For Tom the choice was a simple one; his speech was of course based on his budding love of comedy. When his name was called to speak, Shirley couldn't help but laugh as she watched him saunter up front and center like a cowpoke rustling a herd of cattle. Diving right into his monologue, Tom spent the next few minutes entertaining his classmates with his animated report on comedy. It was at that moment Shirley realized that Tom had a special personality and a gift for telling stories. She wasn't the only one impressed by the humor he incorporated into his speech. The students in the class were in hysterics by the time Tom returned to his desk. "When Tom gave his speech he had the sort of comedian approach," she said, adding that they had to sit him down and tell him to take the project more seriously. "We had to say, 'Now look, you can't be a comedian up there. You've got to give your speech and act fairly straightforward.'"

In the end comedy won out over seriousness; at the age of 12 Tom received his first comedy award, for best overall public speaker in his school. That meant moving to the next level, competing at the school-board finals. Like the other contestants, finalists from schools in the Ottawa area, Tom got up and delivered his speech once again. Only this time he didn't come out the overall winner. The judges gave him kudos for his speaking manner but thought the subject matter was too trivial. For Tom, losing the contest didn't matter, it was the feeling of having command of the entire audience that was thrilling. And now that he had had a taste of it, Tom wanted more.

✳

Grades seven and eight at Henry Munro gave Tom just enough time to hone his comedic skills so that by the time he entered high school he was really ready to take center stage. Just imagine going from a school with only a few hundred students to one with triple that number. He finally had a major audience. It was like hitting the big time. From the moment he set foot on the campus, Tom developed a reputation around Colonel By High School. In between classes, when students were lingering around their lockers, Tom could be found sneaking into the cafeteria kitchen to snatch a plate of pastries to hand out to his friends or bounding through the hallways with endless energy screaming his favorite phrase, "Cheesy chunks, cheesy chunks." Fellow students were usually left to draw the conclusion that he was a little on the bizarre side. As most of the faculty recalls, Tom was always pushing a very fine line between being funny and unique and getting his butt whipped by someone who didn't appreciate his humor. But that didn't deter him from making his cheesy jokes. In fact, after a shopping expedition to the local IGA store, cheese became one of Tom's trademarks. In the dairy aisle, he came across a package of Colby cheese and was intrigued by how similar the name was to his school's name (Colonel By). He thought it was pretty exciting that his school had a dairy product named after it and incorporated it into his routine.

Tom could often be seen entertaining his classmates out in the commons area. He'd put on skateboarding exhibitions with some of his friends while others munched on their lunches. "He was always fearless when it came to acting weird in front of people," said a high school chum. "It was like he was a daredevil, constantly looking for something or someone to react with." His stunts never went unnoticed by students or faculty members. As one longtime office secretary recalls with a stern glance, "Tom spent a lot of time inside the principal's office." And that time wasn't limited to just one school. Living only a few blocks from Colonel By, he would ride his skateboard to class every day. He found that the quickest route to school was straight through the lobby of a local elementary school and out the back door. He'd take off through the playground and make it to homeroom on time. The elementary school was less than appreciative of his skateboard route and put a stop to it by turning him in to the local authorities, who let him off with a warning. "That was sort of the [one and only] brush with the law. He never got into a whole lot of trouble — that we know about," Mary Jane, Tom's mom, explained to Murray Whyte of *Details* magazine.

During the years Tom attended Colonel By, the high school was undergoing a transition. As a younger generation of teachers joined the faculty, the tone of the campus was slowly shifting away from conservative teaching methods to a more individualistic and creative approach. It was at this time that Colonel By alumnus Kerry MacLean joined the staff. Having graduated in the late '70s, Kerry felt a great affinity towards his old alma mater and wanted to bring his family up in the same wholesome community he grew up in. "I just enjoyed my high school life so much that when I decided I wanted to be a teacher I thought it would be pretty great to be back where I came from," said Kerry. What he didn't count on was having Tom Green as a student during his first crack at teaching. He was given duties in science, math, and gym. It was during gym class that he was first able to get a really good impression of the students' individual personalities. Amid the boisterous games of dodgeball and raucous wrestling matches, where most kids are eager to show off their athletic abilities, Tom was distracted, off in his own world.

"His approach to things of course was always loud, boisterous, and attention-grabbing," Kerry MacLean said. "He was so unique that we often were all shocked by what he did." Science class in particular was a place where Tom could show his true colors to fellow classmates. On a number of occasions Kerry caught the young prankster goofing off while he was supposed to be dissecting an insect or performing an experiment. "I'd walk over to his science lab and he'd be chatting with his classmates seriously about the experiment, but he'd be wearing his lab coat backwards and extra pairs of goggles," remembered Kerry. "I always found it very admirable the way he confronted people with ideas that they usually don't talk about in public, or things that people don't usually do. I think he was trying to find a style back then."

Being only 25 at the time, Kerry could identify with Tom's need to break away from the norm. He'd watch the outgoing student, dressed in tennis shoes and a jacket and tie, filming mock Letterman interviews in the hallways with his friends. Where some teachers would have tried to calm Tom's outgoing tendencies, Kerry found his humor refreshing and welcomed it in his classroom. "I was fairly young so I guess my tolerance level was pretty high," he said. "I only really got upset if it was too disruptive to the class." As Tom matured and moved from grade to grade, Kerry watched the impact the young student had on his peers and the atmosphere of the entire school. "What was interesting was how he really looked for ways that he could put his talents to work for the school and of course develop his own abilities," said Kerry.

One of Tom's favorite pastimes was making fun of himself and authority figures. The latter came in handy during math class, where his teacher bore an uncanny resemblance to a celebrity figure from television. The coincidental look-alike gave Tom a plethora of material to use to disrupt the class during boring math equations. "Our grade 10 math teacher looked like Judge Wapner from *The People's Court*," said fellow classmate Ian Thorn. "Tom would goof off in class by standing up and yelling, 'Objection overruled!, Objection overruled!' when he was trying to explain a math problem.'"

Whether he was hanging out with his buddies or poking fun at his teachers, Tom was always keeping a keen eye open for situations he could make fun of. And his high school experiences turned out to be a fruitful source of material for his comedy routine. As soon as Tom had gathered enough material to do a skit, he volunteered to showcase his routine at the school's annual spring and winter concerts. He would do everything from improv skits to emceeing to performing stand-up bits. Whenever he could get up onstage and perform he took the opportunity and thrived on the attention. "The kids around here knew he was very wacky but the energy was infectious," remarked Kerry.

By the time Tom entered his senior years he was well known around the school. The student body was pretty divided when it came to Tom's popularity. Some thought he was funny with a unique personality, while others believed he was completely berserk and just plain strange. "I can remember one night as I was walking home from school that I saw Tom walking home too," said Ian Thorn, recalling the bizarre scene he witnessed. "Tom was walking up the road backwards. He wasn't with anyone, he was alone and just walking backwards. It was weird."

Tom had such a reputation around school that in Grade 11 he decided to capitalize on it and take a political stand by running for student government. Most of his close friends knew these aspirations were motivated by his desire for a captive audience to test out his routines. Tom's fellow candidates took the speeches seriously. They were well prepared and spoke out about needed changes to the school's morale. They tried to get the kids talking about real issues involving the student body. Putting the seriousness aside, Tom got up to deliver his message. He stood up, strolled over to the mike, placed his briefcase on the table in the center of the stage, and waited for a reaction from the audience. Not knowing what to expect next from the "goof-boy," they urged him to speak. Giving in to their demands for a show, Tom threw open his briefcase and whipped out some kitchen utensils and vegetables he'd stolen from his mom's refrigerator and started to throw together a tossed salad. The teachers and students stared in amazement, not knowing what to make of the crazy guy onstage. By the time Tom finished his salad preparations he had the majority of the students laughing in their seats and a few of the faculty members shaking their heads in disbelief at the mockery he'd made of the assembly.

Getting a good taste of the impact he could have on his audience simply by doing what came naturally, he followed up his salad toss with an appearance at a Colonel By Air Bands competition. While the groups took to the stage strumming their imaginary guitars, Tom had other things on his mind. Walking out onto the stage with a dozen eggs and a hot frying pan, he entertained the audience between sets with a comedic cooking segment. "I think people expect me to do something weird," he told reporter Denis Grignon at the time. While most people were laughing at the contrast between Green and his fellow students, some were shocked at his blatant disregard for the rules. "It was too far out," said Kerry, chuckling at the memory of Tom onstage. "It made people wonder what he was all about. It made people think that if he can't get his act together and say something, then forget it. But what they didn't realize was that he was so far ahead of his time."

Performing in front of an audience had really piqued Tom's interest by Grade 13 and he used every opportunity to test his abilities. It was in English class that friends saw Tom's innate talent for acting. The class was broken into several small groups and given an assignment to discuss one of Shakespeare's plays. For Tom and his group, which included his buddies Derek Harvie and Ian Lewer, just reading a soliloquy wasn't good enough. They were eager to make a lasting impression on their English teacher and fellow classmates — a goal which soon found the group in a very unusual situation. Under Tom's outrageous leadership, the group dressed themselves in Shakespearean garb and snuck through the back passages leading to the rooftop of the Sheraton Hotel in Ottawa. "It was really strange how it all happened," said Ian Lewer. "We were on the roof waving around pretend swords and videotaping ourselves throwing a squash off the roof" — which, Ian remarked, really had nothing to do with the play they were working on. "He really used his creativity and artistic license."

✱

By the ripe old age of 17, Tom was ready to test out his material on real paying customers. For amateurs wanting to break into the Ottawa comedy scene, that means signing up for Mark Breslin's Yuk Yuk's Komedy Kabaret. On the small platform stage young comedians are initiated into the ranks on amateur nights. Every Thursday evening, after the seasoned professionals dazzle the fans, the fresh-faced, vulnerable wanna-bes take to the stage hoping to follow in their mentors' footsteps. There's no screening or censoring process for amateurs wanting to try their hand at stand-up; the only prerequisites are to phone ahead to book a performance time and to prepare a six-minute routine that is, ideally, clever and funny. For some, stand-up is a hobby to pass the time. For others it's their lifelong ambition; they love the thrill of entertaining and delight in the sounds of laughter from the crowd. For Tom

Green, amateur night was a way to escape from the reality of being a geeky teenager and walk tenderfooted into his dream world. On the lonely stage in the dark basement below what was once the Beacon Arms Hotel, Tom exposed his true personality for the benefit of the audience.

Grabbing the mike the first time, Tom looked skeptically out into the faces of the 150 or so people seated in the audience anxiously waiting for the act to begin. As if sensing Tom's fears, a few disbelievers could be heard snickering in the silence. Tom knew he was going to have his work cut out for him if he wanted to win over the audience. Giving the once-over to the people sitting in the first row, he wondered if they'd be critiquing his routine, like he'd done to other performers. After all, it was only a short time before his Yuk Yuk's debut that Tom and his pal Phil Giroux had come into the comedy club and heckled the performers, much to the dismay of the club's owners. "We actually had to throw him out one night," says Yuk Yuk's manager Howard Wagman. "Tom came across as a smart-ass kid, but you could tell he was very bright and unique."

Standing on the stage, Tom took a deep breath and straightened the jacket-and-tie combo he was wearing (seemingly snagged right out of his dad's closet) before he launched into his routine. It was filled with jokes about the ironies of life as a teenager and the dilemmas he faced, like borrowing his parents' car and sneaking out past curfew. Looking out from under the bright stage lights through the smoke-filled room, Tom spouted off a few lines. "What?! I hear you have to have ID to buy stuff now," he shouted out while bounding across the stage. Stopping, he stared out into the audience and they caught a glimpse of his face, scrunched up so his eyeballs bulged out, looking twice their normal size. Breathing a sigh of relief, Tom could hear the sound of laughter pounding in his eardrums. His performance was raw but unique, and it struck a chord with the crowd and actually made them laugh. That was pretty much all Tom was looking for.

From the moment he stepped out onto the stage Tom knew he had found his calling. The years of pestering his classmates with one-liners and interrogating his parents on a daily basis about whether or not a joke would bomb finally felt worthwhile. As he gained more experience performing in comedy clubs, Tom's material became more polished. He learned from other comedians the necessity of timing in the delivery of a joke and how to interact with the crowd. The more often he appeared onstage, the more noticeably passionate he discovered he was about entertaining. He thrived on the attention and loved being in the spotlight. Eventually just appearing on amateur night and at high school events wasn't enough. He needed to test his talents on a bigger audience to see if he had what it took to make a career in show business.

2

TOMFOOLERY

Comedy came naturally to Tom, but what happened by accident was his affinity for music. He stumbled onto it one evening while emceeing an assembly at Colonel By High School. Between introducing the different guests, Tom strayed from his regular stand-up routine and started doing some rhyming phrases. By the end of the assembly he had hammered out some lyrics and constructed an accompanying beat. Afterwards, he hurried home to work on more material. The ideas came flooding to him and the addition of music inspired his writing. He had a new hobby he loved, and, to his parents' delight, Tom was finally up and out of the house looking for summer jobs to help finance his work. Every spare dollar he had went to buying keyboards, samplers, and skateboards. When he wasn't in the basement creating beats, he could be found out on the street entertaining the neighborhood kids by doing tricks on the skateboard ramps he'd constructed. He always attracted a large crowd of fans with his fearless antics; to his audience's amazement, Tom would twist his gangly frame into weird shapes as he jumped the ramps.

He made so much of an impression on his fellow classmates that there was a special dedication to him in the 1988 Colonel By yearbook. A picture of Tom skateboarding appeared with an inscription: "A bizarre legion of beings has invaded the school . . . Junior skaters. Until last year the most visible member of the skateboarding cult was our one and only Tom Green, but with the advent of September we were introduced

Tom was already turning the world upside down (1988)
COURTESY SHANNON HAWKINS

to many more of them. Will they stay true to their skater roots, or will their boards be left in musty closets?"

While establishing the skateboarding club, Tom developed a rapport with many of the younger students at the school. Greg Campbell, who was three years younger than Tom, shared his love of skateboarding and music. Even though there was a big age difference the two became fast friends. "We had a lot in common, but skateboarding was a passion for both of us," said Greg.

But Tom had other plans for him and his new friend. Having gotten a rush from performing some of his rap music onstage, Tom set his sights on a higher-profile performance — the annual holiday presentation. "He asked me if I could rap and if I wanted to put something together with him for the Christmas concert," said Greg, who was only 14 at the time. Being an avid musician himself, Greg grabbed at the chance to perform. Soon they invited another high school pal, Geordie Ferguson, into their group. The trio spent weeks holed up in the basement of their parents' homes. While Greg and Tom worked on the lyrics, Geordie was the DJ. "We started out just having fun in a really crazy environment," said

Greg, recalling the days they spent developing their own style of hip-hop. "It was a blast!" In fact their Christmas concert went over so well that the group decided to try out their act on the general public. Tom had already gathered a lot of experience on comedy club stages so he knew what entertaining was all about. "We just kept doing more shows around town," said Greg. "We used to do shows at Barrymore's [a bar] and enter talent contests at the Ex [Central Canada Exhibition]. It seemed to be going somewhere and we all loved it."

Shortly after the teen group started to make the rounds, they found themselves sharing the stage with some of the biggest Canadian rap bands of the time. They were up against some hard-core rappers, and Tom, Greg, and Geordie stood out like a sore thumb. Their rap music was entirely different from what other musicians were coming out with. The trio had a distinct sound and lyrical flavor that wasn't about making a political statement. Their lyrics were a refreshing change of pace — they were humorous. "We were on the stage entertaining the audience with what were essentially jokes and entertaining ourselves at the same time," said Greg.

After a few short months the threesome developed a following among rap fans in Ottawa and were frequently asked to perform in bars and clubs. Things seemed to be happening quickly; the group was so new on the scene that they hadn't even had the time to come up with a name for their band. "We were sitting in class one day discussing the fact that no one knew what to call us, so we all suggested a few names," said Greg. "A girl in the class suggested Organized Rhyme and it stuck." From that moment on Tom, Greg, and Geordie had a name, and they began to think of themselves as a bona fide group — they were Organized Rhyme.

Away from the stage the three skateboarding friends were typical teenagers, outfitted in baggy jeans and T-shirts and blending in with their classmates at Colonel By, but onstage they were able to express their individuality through their music. Entertaining became an outlet for their creativity. At the time the Ottawa music scene was fueled by live music venues that showcased local talent. It was commonplace for bars to give new bands the chance to appear onstage Thursday, Friday, and Saturday evenings to test their skills in front of a crowd. As soon as

Organized Rhyme had their lyrics and beats worked out, they set out to wow audiences with their humor. Every aspect of their stage presence incorporated joking around, from the dancers onstage grooving to their beat to the props they used in each set. "Every show was so different because it was, like, what we were about at that exact moment," Greg said speaking of one show where the group was totally off-the-wall. "We all [dancers and band] came out with baskets on our heads and we handed out doorknobs to the audience." Encouraged by loud cheers from the bar crowd, the band soon realized that the more outrageous they got, the louder the applause was. "We were both pretty serious about wanting to be noticed and freak people out," explained Greg of the thrill he and Tom enjoyed from catching people by surprise. People came to the Organized Rhyme show expecting serious rappers and ended up spending the evening in hysterics.

The mayhem Organized Rhyme created onstage helped to solidify their personas. With Tom's wiry frame he was known as Bones, Geordie's masterful work as DJ saw him nicknamed DJ Signal, and Greg borrowed the nickname Pin the Chameleon from a disturbing character in a horror flick. Now they had the whole act together and were really beginning to feel their way through the mechanics of performing. Organized Rhyme snatched up every gig they could get around town and were quickly becoming a hot commodity for promoters. "They were so off-the-wall and had very good rhythm," said Ottawa booking agent and colorful lounge singer Johnny Vegas. "What really impressed me was that these white guys could really rap. To me, coming from a musical background where I sing Frank Sinatra and Tony Bennett, that these guys could rap seemed like a novelty."

It wasn't only the music that had fans jammed into the local clubs — it was their comical stage performances too. During one of their first gigs at the Downstairs Club, Organized Rhyme opened for Ottawa band Furnaceface. Traditionally an opening act is onstage to warm up the audience for the main event, but in Organized Rhyme's case they worked the room like they were the main attraction and veteran musicians. For the 30-minute set the audience was mesmerized by the young rappers. They looked innocent enough, but, as the audience soon realized, this was no ordinary stage performance. The group jumped onto the stage with a large crate. As the crowd packed into the bar, Tom, Geordie, and Greg got themselves psyched for their act. Tom stripped off his sneakers and paraded out onto the stage to the applause of the crowd. Their support was enough to get him into character as Geordie started up the beat. Greg was the first to chime in with the lyrics as Tom disappeared behind the crate. Then, out of nowhere, pieces of Wonder Bread went flying across the stage and out into the mass of people hovering close to the small platform.

"It was hilarious because the people didn't quite know what to make of it," recalled Tom Stewart, bass player for Furnaceface. He and the rest of his band watched the show from the wings. Furnaceface had been choreographing shows like the Organized Rhyme stunt, looking to shock audiences, and they were duly impressed by the creativity. It brought back feelings of nostalgia for earlier shows Furnaceface had worked on; during one set, Stewart was outfitted with a silver nylon suit that would inflate during the song, transforming him into punk-rocking Michelin Man. "It gives the audiences something to talk about after the show is over. It's a conversation piece," said Stewart. As the bread Tom had been throwing out into the crowd formed a gooey, crusty, beer-soaked layer on the floor, Organized Rhyme launched into a satirical song about being three white teens from suburbia and making it in the world of rap music. They called themselves Wonder Boys — hence the shopping spree for 24 loaves of day-old Wonder Bread from the grocery store. In the midst of the chaos Tom pranced around the stage getting bread mashed between his toes and up the sides of his legs. "It looked like he was wearing clogs," explained Stewart. "His feet were covered about three inches thick with soggy bread."

As the audience applauded this outlandish behavior, the band spiraled further out of control. If Greg or Tom would miss a line in a rap the other would order him to do a set of push-ups. Organized Rhyme were a hit by the time they finally walked off the stage to make way for the headliners. The spontaneous humor of the group had caught the audience off guard and endeared the young band to them. What the teen rappers didn't realize was that there was a very special person sitting in the audience taking notes about their set. He saw raw talent in Organized Rhyme and wanted to know more about where these guys came from.

✳

Organized Rhyme's first big break in developing a real fan base, apart from playing the club scene, came from Bob McCarthy, the programming director at the University of Ottawa's CHUO radio station. After a brainstorming session with the staff at the station, Bob was sold on the idea of bringing in a radio DJ to host a rap music show. There was only one catch: he wanted the host to be involved in the industry, preferably someone who was already part of an established group. He was gambling that the station's ratings would increase if he brought in a band to host the program, because they would bring their fans along with them.

When McCarthy saw Organized Rhyme take to the stage he was hooked on their performance and knew that with their outgoing personalities and youthful energy they would be perfect for the volunteer job. Their humor was just outrageous enough to transcend age barriers, and would interest both university and high school crowds. By the time McCarthy had the opportunity to ask Tom and Greg to host the Friday night program, which ran from midnight to 2 a.m., the pair were looking for something new to work on. They'd been performing live and developing a name around town, but they wanted to capitalize on the hype surrounding their group. They were in search of more exposure and the chance to host a radio show seemed to be the perfect solution.

Tom threw himself into the new project from the very beginning. It was an opportunity to show audiences what he had to offer as an entertainer and the station was willing to give him some room to develop his skills. Being new to the job, he was keen to get involved in every aspect of the radio program, from engineering and development to marketing and promotions. As the show hit the airwaves, Tom could be found during the week designing his own posters. He'd walk around town tacking them to telephone poles or handing them out at diners and bus stops. The posters would give potential listeners info about *The Rap Show*'s time slot and musical selections. Across the bottom he'd put head shots of what he identified as himself and Greg — only they weren't their own photos, but rather ones of uptight-looking businessmen. "It was great," says former CHUO station manager Karen McHarg, who first met Tom Green when she was a sales director there. "His comedy was ingenious." Tom made such a great impression on the young sales associate that she helped to forward his career at the station every chance she got. "Every time someone called in to complain and they wanted to get rid of him I'd say, 'C'mon, that's Tom Green, he's one of the best!'"

Tom's career as a rap DJ took off as his voice boomed into the mike. Through word of mouth his popularity spread like wildfire as people discussed his late-night endeavors. "Did you hear that guy Green on the radio?" fans of the show would ask in local bars. "Can you believe he gets away with doing that kind of stuff on the air?"

As his experience in the booth grew, so too did his penchant for entertaining audiences. *The Rap Show*, initially developed to highlight rap bands and local artists, soon gathered momentum as a comedy spot. Each week Tom invented creative ways to entertain his audience. For one Friday evening he planned a show that left his listeners guessing all weekend long; some were even a little agitated. Inside the studio he played one song over and over again for the entire two hours of his show; meanwhile, inside the studio's audition booth he taped his own live broadcast. Listeners could only hear the live show when Tom cut in to take phone calls from irate fans. "You're playing the same song over and over. Something is wrong," they informed the host. Tom would respond in all sincerity that there must be something wrong with their radios because he was playing a different song. Callers on the line would hear in the background of their conversation the songs he was playing inside the audition booth, which of course were different from what was playing across the airwaves. Listening to the taped show at home, Karen was doubled over with laughter as she heard the intent fans trying to convince Tom he was repeating the same song. "Tom would argue with them that they were crazy and I think some would actually start believing him," she said.

Tom's first real stab at independence was to move away from home and enroll at college. He saw a natural progression from his love for entertaining to the broadcasting industry. In the fall of 1991 he started a two-year television broadcasting course at Algonquin College in Ottawa. His stay at the school, however, was short-lived; at the end of the semester he dropped out to pursue his musical career. The members of

Organized Rhyme, which had started out as three guys just goofing around at their high school assemblies, found themselves on a train bound for the bright lights of New York City. A producer who had enthusiastically watched a couple of their live appearances in Ottawa was so impressed with the act that he wanted to help them put together their first music video. For two weeks the group toured the Big Apple between studio recording sessions. "It was a lot of fun because we were still so young," explains Greg Campbell. "In the end our partnership with the producer didn't work out but we were able to make a video and check out the New York artistic scene."

✶

While working on the radio show and frequently playing the local club scene, Organized Rhyme was given another golden opportunity to take their act to a larger audience. Another Canadian band, the Dream Warriors, had just returned from a European tour and were headlining a live concert in Halifax. An Ottawa promoter had contacted Organized Rhyme to book them as the opening act. Tom, Greg, and Geordie were ecstatic. It would be their biggest show to date. After convincing their parents the show was a career-defining moment and would be beneficial to their future as musicians, the group agreed to play the Halifax date. There was only one condition — Greg's parents were to accompany the band on their adventure. "Greg was still pretty young at the time. Although we wanted to support his creativity, we wanted to be there for assistance if he needed it," said Greg's dad, Hugh. The Campbell family car was packed up and the group headed out east to Halifax.

It was the end of the summer and the weather was perfect for the two-car caravan to make the long drive. With Greg, Tom, and Geordie in his car, Hugh couldn't help but get caught up in their excitement. For the entire trip the boys sat in the back talking about girls and humming lyrics. By the time they reached their destination, a venue they recalled as the Flamingo Club, the adrenaline was pumping through their young veins. "It was their coming-out show and in hindsight I think they all knew it was going to change their lives," said Hugh. They left their teenage personalities at the door and entered the portal leading to adulthood.

Bouncing into the trendy club the boys were ready to put on a show. They had a cockiness that could only be categorized by veteran musicians as naivete. They had a very important job ahead of them, and, depending on the success of the show, their futures could be changed dramatically. Word had filtered down to them after rehearsals that there would be some very influential promoters and critics watching the show. They desperately needed to make a lasting impression on these people if they wanted the band to move to the next level.

Before the show began, Organized Rhyme hung out backstage learning everything they could about the music industry from Toronto's Dream Warriors and their manager, Ivan Berry. They were well known in the Canadian music industry, and, like Organized Rhyme, were breaking ground with their expansion of traditional music theory. The Dream Warriors were on the cutting edge of a sub-genre of rap music they described coincidentally as organized rhyme, a blending of rap, jazz, and hip-hop. With hit songs like "Wash Your Face in My Sink" and "Day In Day Out" under their belt, they were awe-inspiring to Tom, Greg, and Geordie. A few minutes before being introduced to the crowd, Tom walked over to Ivan Berry and suggested he check out Organized Rhyme's performance. He vowed it would be one of the weirdest shows Berry had ever seen. A moment later Tom disappeared from backstage only to reappear hanging from the rafters as Greg and Geordie started the beat. "The show just blew me away," said Berry. "They were so talented and really, really funny."

As Tom leapt from the overhang to join Greg and Geordie onstage, Berry watched from backstage in amazement. The comedian picked up a box of pizza and dished out the cheesy treat to the throng of fans lining the platform. "Cheesy, cheesy," Tom cried out in character. Ivan sat back in his chair with his eyes glued to Organized Rhyme as they launched into a few of their beats. He listened intently to the screams from young girls in the crowd pledging their love for the music and the teen rappers. After Organized Rhyme's opening set wrapped up and the Dream Warriors took control of the show, Tom, Greg, and Geordie slipped inconspicuously into the wings. Getting up from his chair to greet the rappers, Berry knew he had just witnessed something special and started making plans for the future.

*

At the same time as Tom was doing *The Rap Show* on Friday evenings, Glenn Humplik was manning CHUO's call-in show, *Nightfall*, from 2 to 6 a.m. It wasn't long before the two radio hosts, both working grave-yard shifts, became close friends and collaborated on ideas for both of their shows. The connection they made was instantaneous. Tom was as fearless as Glenn was conservative. They played well off each other on the air. Having done the rap program and, in contrast, the call-in radio show, it was apparent that Tom's love of goofing off was prevailing over his musical interests. He thrived on the interaction with listeners and loved the spontaneity of live radio so much that he lobbied the program-ming director for his own call-in show. A few months later *Midnight Caller* was born. It was Tom's baby from the start and combined his love of entertaining, music, and humor all under one umbrella. On Friday evenings he'd switch on the mike and fall into his own little world. Since CHUO did not have a delay system to filter out unsavory comments, everyone listening was quickly sucked into his world. "There was always a concern that something would go on the air that was politically incor-rect, but I'd listen from home and just laugh all evening," said Karen McHarg.

Listeners were drawn to *Midnight Caller* because of the element of surprise it always offered. You never knew quite what was going to hap-pen from week to week, which, as Karen describes, was one of the things that endeared Tom to his listeners. Just to prove the point, one Friday evening Tom did the entire broadcast from a cell phone, snuggled in bed between his parents as they tried to fall asleep. "On the air you could hear the Greens in the background saying, 'Tom why don't you just get up and go down to the station, *please*!'" Karen said.

In between songs and stunts Tom would spend most of his broad-cast bantering back and forth with callers on a wide variety of topics, from local bands to news events. "He got his kicks out of making fun of callers or hanging up on them just to see how they would react," recalled Karen. During one call with a listener Tom started asking her an array of weird questions, like what color the carpet was in her house and what items she had in her refrigerator. In fact, he was so smitten that he decided to take the show on the road and drive across town to her Orleans home. Grabbing a cell phone, he hopped into his car and drove to her neighborhood to continue the interview. The only thing he forgot before leaving the station was to get directions to her house. He called the station from his cell phone to ask one of the guys to call the girl back and get directions. Not knowing he was still live on the air at the time, Tom said he was going to stop at the Petro-Canada gas station in Orleans and await their instructions.

By the time he drove up to the service center he was greeted by a handful of fans all holding up Ottawa maps. "They had heard the broadcast and that he was a bit lost and went to try and help," laughed Karen. After greeting the small group of eager listeners, he figured out the quickest route to the caller's home and led the convoy to her address. The five or so cars parked on the street while Tom went inside to wake up her sleeping parents and finish the broadcast. "At one point the cars outside were honking their horns and flashing their lights so that Tom had to go on the air asking them to keep it down outside until he finished the interview," Karen said, remarking on how phenomenal the response to Midnight Caller was. "One of the most interesting revelations about Tom's show was the number of people who would call in over the weekend freaking out. They wouldn't be the ones that he'd made fun of on the air, but rather the people that he hadn't been able to put on the show. They were mad because he hadn't made fun of them."

Over the years of working at CHUO Tom Green became synonymous with outrageous behavior. And it would be commonplace for him to encourage his fans to follow suit. It became a ritual that during his sign-off he would invite listeners to meet him on Parliament Hill at 2 a.m for a rousing game of soccer. "You wouldn't believe it but he'd show up on the Hill and there would be 20 or 30 people there waiting to play a game. It was amazing," said Karen, adding that after the first few soccer matches Tom added the stipulation that they had to bring him doughnuts. "It was a lot of fun to just listen to him coming up with these ideas."

It was only a few weeks after Tom, Greg, and Geordie returned home from their debut concert in Halifax that their lives took a drastic turn. During an evening rehearsal in Greg's basement the group received a

phone call from Dream Warriors manager Ivan Berry. Berry was so captivated and impressed with Organized Rhyme's Halifax performance
that he was requesting they come out to Toronto's Wellesley Studio to
record their first album. "Oh my God, could this really be happening?"
the group asked one another when they got the news. Just think of it —
girls flocking around the stage screaming in adoration and young kids
waiting around backstage after a performance to ask for autographs. It
was almost too much to absorb at the time. As the trio went on dreaming about their futures, Berry continued on with his proposal. Having
just launched a new label, Boombastic, produced under Berry's Beat
Factory on A&M Records, he was looking for fresh talent to record as
the label's first release. He wanted something inventive and full of
imagination, like nothing else on the market — qualities he knew Organized Rhyme possessed. "It was soooo cool. We went to Toronto and
recorded some demo stuff and ended up with a record contract,"
explained Greg Campbell. "For us it was kind of easy because we had
tons of material, but we never released anything 'cause we just did live
shows. So we had a lot to work with."

After months of recording, Organized Rhyme released their first album,
Huh!? Stiffenin' Against the Wall. Their repertoire covered anything and
everything they came in contact with. "In the studio we would just throw
stuff out and no matter how abstract or hilarious, we'd go with it," Greg
said, explaining their musical style. The outcome of their first album
was a collection of songs such as "Papercuts," "Cookies and Crackers,"
and "The Rain Song." On many of the tracks they had collaborated with
fellow rappers Dream Warriors, LA Love, and Blast. "Their music was
about everyday occurrences," said Berry, chuckling to himself as he
explained how the group used their mascot, the armadillo, as the subject
of one of their songs. "They would rap about how fucked-up and slow
the armadillo is."

In 1992 Organized Rhyme released "Check the OR," the first single
and video off their debut album. The video, directed by Tim Hamilton,
won a MuchMusic video award and featured a cameo appearance by
King Lou, a member of the Dream Warriors. The concept for the video
was that Organized Rhyme went in search of where Lou came from.
Tom, Greg, and Geordie walked the streets of Toronto's tough Jane and

Finch area looking for Lou, but they were denied access to the projects by a band of thugs. En route, the group went through a grocery store trying to pretend they were hard-core rappers, but they just ended up throwing stuff around. "It was just, like, turn the cameras on and let the fools go," laughed Berry. Being Canadian talent and a hit with rap fans, "Check the OR" found its way onto MuchMusic's weekly video rotation.

The momentum that had helped to launch their careers continued. "It was like living with a pop star in the house," said Hugh Campbell. "There were always giggling girls calling and asking to talk with Greg. It never stopped." For the Campbell household, the success Greg was experiencing had its ups and downs. His parents wanted him to reach his potential and if music was his passion they encouraged his endeavors, but they were a little leery about the choice he had made of rap music. "When the rap craze came along, most parents weren't thrilled with their kids doing rap," Hugh explained. "Some of it was really rough stuff." After watching Greg and Tom let loose onstage he was able to set aside most of his doubts. Hugh was overjoyed that the kids had found a positive outlet for their energy.

As "Check the OR" received more airplay, the band soon found themselves being scheduled for more and more appearances. Suddenly they were doing real paying gigs and signed on to be the stars of a Loeb pizza commercial. The group was paid a fee of $7,500 for acting in the TV spot. They were finally beginning to reap the rewards of all their hard work. But this was just the beginning — the music industry had bigger things in store for this little rap group from Ottawa. Ironically, however, just as their music careers started to soar, their interests in music began to shift, and the only question remaining was if Organized Rhyme could withstand the pressure of change.

✳

Their success had been quick and exciting, but Organized Rhyme was not prepared for the level of respect they received from the Canadian music industry. In 1992 they were nominated for a Juno Award, Canada's answer to the Grammys. The Juno Awards, a celebration of excellence in Canadian music, were established in 1970 as strictly an industry event.

They were founded by Walt Grealis and Stan Klees, the publishers of
RPM *Weekly,* a music-trade magazine, as a way of bringing industry
recognition to Canadian artists and their music. In 1975, the Junos were
brought to the forefront of the music industry when the Canadian Acad-
emy of Recording Arts and Sciences was established and began to
televise the annual awards ceremony. As the Juno Awards have continued to grow, so too has the success of its recipients, who have included
Shania Twain, Alanis Morissette, Celine Dion, The Tragically Hip, and
many more high-profile artists over the years. A Juno is something most
Canadian artists work towards all their careers. For Organized Rhyme,
the nomination had come without them even thinking to expect it. After
all, the band's main goal was to act crazy in front of other people. They
didn't take themselves too seriously for fear their audience might follow
suit.

Organized Rhyme's "Check the OR" was nominated in the best rap
category. They were in good company alongside "Keep it Slammin'" by
Devon, "The Jungle Man" by the Maximum Definition, "The Maestro
Zone" by Maestro Fresh Wes, and "Really Livin'" by Ragga Muffin
Rascals. The ceremony was held on March 21, 1993, at what was then
the O'Keefe Centre in downtown Toronto. Tom and Greg attended the
festivities alongside the other nominees. While most artists go through
pangs of anxiety wondering whether or not they'll bring home the
award, Organized Rhyme were ecstatic to simply be in the room. Just
getting to this point was icing on the cake. Don't get the wrong idea,
though — they went expecting to win. Entering the concert hall for the
22nd annual Juno Awards ceremony, Greg and Tom soon found themselves rubbing elbows with some of Canada's top musicians. Alannah
Myles, Kim Mitchell, Blue Rodeo, and The Tragically Hip were among
the nominees that evening. Finding their seats in the theater, Greg put
aside his anxious feelings about the award, allowing himself to soak in
the environment around him. Years later he recalled the evening as if it
happened only yesterday. "We sat down and looked around and there
was Corey Hart seated behind us and one of the guys from Skid Row at
our side," he said.

By the time the house lights dimmed and Quebec songstress Celine
Dion took to the stage as emcee, tensions were mounting around the

room as everyone speculated on winners for the evening. Dion had received nods in several categories including entertainer of the year, best Francophone album, album of the year, and two entries in the single of the year division and was calm onstage despite all the attention. Halfway through the program the presenters finally arrived at the category for best rap. "And the nominees are," the voices rang out through the building, "'Check the OR,' Organized Rhyme; 'Keep it Slammin',' Devon . . ." Greg and Tom wriggled in their seats anticipating the rush to the stage they were about to make. "And the winner is," the announcer called out. "Keep it Slammin'" by Devon." Greg sank down in his plush seat as he watched Devon graciously accept his award. "We should have won," Greg said to himself. "We should have won."

They appeared to be on the cusp of national success, but losing the Juno may have been an omen of things to come for Organized Rhyme. As more opportunities popped up, they found the focus of their music beginning to change. They were being asked to act more like hard-core rappers rather than the jokesters they really were. The silver shine of their music career was beginning to tarnish. "The whole atmosphere was gone and we weren't doing as many jokes anymore. It was too serious," admitted Greg, the melancholy apparent in his voice.

"It was like, 'Oh, we've got a record deal now, we're rappers and should be hard-core. The comedy thing was just flipped away." It was a tough time for the band and they felt as though they were being pulled in several different directions, with no real path to follow. The record label wanted Organized Rhyme to go through a transition from funny to serious rappers, building on their sound for a follow-up album. Unfortunately, it was no longer what the group desired. They'd grown apart and the differences in their personalities were evident. "We all learned a little bit about each other and we just kind of got turned off somehow," Greg explained about the reason for the group's decision to split in 1993. "The music changed."

Tom, Greg, and Geordie decided to go their separate ways. Geordie ventured off to university in London, Ontario. Meanwhile, Greg signed up for the television broadcasting course at Algonquin College, but his love of music was too strong; he lasted three days before he quit and moved to Vancouver to open up his own studio, BigStuff Productions.

Tom decided to make a second attempt at the Algonquin television broadcasting course, as a kind of escape from having to start looking for a job. This time he was determined to focus all his energies on finishing the course and establishing his career in entertainment.

3

DIVING IN

Jumping fully clothed into the water fountain outside the Nepean mayor's office, Tom picked up a live lobster from a carrying case and puckered his lips. "Roll the camera," Algonquin College broadcasting student Darcy De Toni said to the cameraman. A small group of students watched in amazement as classmate Tom Green sprang to life. "He was going completely crazy," recalled De Toni. "He started talking to the lobster, saying, 'I'm going to kiss you, I'm going to kiss you.'" For more than half an hour, Tom splashed around the fountain making outrageous gestures towards the slippery critter. "The lobster wants to bite my face," he wailed to the crowd as he ran through the pool holding the lobster behind him in a mock chase. Laughter erupted from the crowd gathered to watch the antics and it got louder as the building security guard approached the small film crew. "You're going to have to leave. Get out of that fountain!" the guard yelled in Tom's direction. Still holding the lobster, Tom emerged from the water, soaking wet and bubbling over with excitement. "Did you get all that?" Tom asked the cameraman. "That was perfect!"

As Darcy stood in the background watching Tom discuss the situation with the security guard, he was struck by Tom's fearless nature. Rushing back to campus, the group edited their short lobster parody and prepared it for classroom viewing. It was one of the first projects the Algonquin broadcasting students had produced for their professor, and they were eager to find out what he thought of their work. Although the assignment wasn't technically perfect, it was one of the most memorable times in their lives. Tom had made it exciting, and it was just the beginning.

"I always thought Tom was pretty crazy," said Darcy, thinking back to the first time he met Tom at college. "For little video projects he was always out of control." Darcy chose a quieter, behind-the-scenes role in broadcasting — he had dreams of becoming the producer of his own show. With only a handful of network stations in Ottawa and only one year of broadcasting school to his credit, getting his foot in the door seemed like a pipe dream to Darcy. Hoping to gain some valuable experience, he signed up as a volunteer at Rogers Community TV station in Ottawa. In the spring of 1994 he began his volunteer apprenticeship at Rogers and worked alongside staff producer and director Ray Hagel on a comedy program.

After working on the show for a few weeks, Darcy went back to his broadcasting class and suggested that the students create their own show to gain experience. He talked it over with fellow production-class member Trevor Cavanagh, and the pair decided on a mock late-night talk show, an idea that had come from a term project. Each student had been asked to write a proposal for a TV program and Trevor's had a talk-show format. Brainstorming with fellow classmates about the idea one afternoon, they decided that they would ask Tom Green to host the program. They'd all heard his radio program, *Midnight Caller,* on CHUO, the University of Ottawa's radio station, and thought his material was hilarious. "There was this one segment he called 'Crazy Classifieds' that had me in stitches," said Darcy. In the segment Tom opens up a local newspaper to the classified section and calls people at random to ask them bizarre questions about the objects they've listed for sale. Tom had an endless supply of energy and, as they had witnessed in class projects, he had an outrageous personality. Without wasting any time, Trevor and Darcy approached Tom with the idea of taking his radio show to television and starting their own late-night talk show. Tom jumped at the opportunity and was bursting with ideas for the show.

The three broadcasting pals met the following week to design the look for *The Tom Green Show,* which they would pitch to Rogers for the fall lineup. Darcy and Tom met with Trevor in his parents' basement to sketch out a plan for the show. It would be built on a foundation of unpredictability that Tom would expand on each week. The bulk of the program would be developed along the lines of a typical late-night talk show, but with a twist — they planned to intertwine guest segments with prerecorded clips of Tom interacting with people on the street.

Tom decided his outrageous humor would have the biggest impact if he had a sidekick/cohost on the couch beside him. The person would have to be equally as outrageous, but from the other side of the spectrum — so incredibly normal and mainstream that the audience would see a drastic contrast between host and cohost. Tom offered to ask one of his good friends, Glenn Humplik, to act the part. The two had met a few years earlier on another CHUO radio show, *Nightfall*, where they had discovered they played well off each other. "We realized that having two people playing off each other would work better than just having one person talking to the crowd," explained Trevor Cavanagh. Soon Glenn was on board as the faithful sidekick, with the stipulation that he would play a small role in the show's overall development. After all, he had his own career to focus on.

Once that was settled they set out to design the nuts and bolts of the program. They wanted the set to have a low-budget feel to ensure that guests and audience members would not feel intimidated by their surroundings. To reflect the crazy, unpredictable atmosphere of the show, the furniture would be hanging upside down from the ceiling. The bizarre set, combined with what they called "irrelevant background events," would hold the audience's attention from the moment they tuned in or arrived at the studio. That's where Phil Giroux came into play. He would sit in the window behind Tom's desk sipping coffee and laughing at offbeat moments. But his character didn't originally have such an obvious role on the show; it grew out of one of his personality traits. Once the guys heard his unmistakable, boisterous laugh they came up with an idea. In order to get the audience psyched about the live tapings, they planted Phil and his one-of-a-kind chuckle in the seats and would intermittently shove the camera in his face for a reaction. Eventually his character began to develop. "He'd laugh at what other people didn't find funny," commented Trevor. "And his laugh was so loud and had a connotation of being self-centered and egotistical that he was eventually

Tom cooks up some juicy laughs on the early Tom Green Show *(1994)*
COURTESY ROGERS COMMUNITY TELEVISION

incorporated into the irrelevant background events of the show's format."

Phil's semi-obnoxious, ladies'-man persona, coupled with Tom's outlandish pranks and Glenn's real-man integrity, helped to fulfill the
show's mandate: to be "like a piece of spinach caught in someone's
teeth." The three aspiring producers, Tom, Trevor, and Darcy, summa-
rized the show: "At times *The Tom Green Show* is uncomfortable to look
at but for some indescribable reason you can't stop watching it."

*

Ray Skaff arrived at the Rogers offices on Richmond Road in Ottawa,
prepared for another busy day, which included a meeting with his produc-

tion staff to go over new ideas for the fall schedule. When he reached his office his eyes immediately locked onto a large object taking up a good part of the desk. "What the heck is that?" he asked aloud, moving towards the table. "A pineapple? What's going on here?" He interrogated the fruit as if expecting a response. Examining the pineapple more closely, he noticed a package of papers lying beside it with a cassette. "Proposal for *The Tom Green Show,*" the cover letter read, and a smile crossed Ray's face. "Very creative," he thought. "It's quirky and attention-grabbing. Not bad."

Tom, Darcy, and Trevor had sent three pineapples to Rogers along with a grade-school picture of Tom and a note reading, "Looking forward to meeting you." One went to Ray Skaff, another to Colette Watson, the director of programming for the Eastern Region, and the third to Karen Pickles, head of programming development at the station. The stunt was designed to grab their attention and get them talking about the show's proposal, and it worked.

Being a community cable station, Rogers gets a number of proposals every year from people wanting to start up their own television show. It's Ray and Karen's job to choose those people they want to develop as new talent for the upcoming fall schedule. The key for Rogers is to accept those entries that would make the biggest impact on their audiences, offering something new in terms of entertainment. Ray was looking to change the way viewers perceive cable television. Gone were the days when an old black-velvet curtain hung loosely over a studio stage as untrained actors presented their work. The cable station of the 1990s would work to compete with mainstream broadcasters by offering viewers in-depth local coverage, all the while nurturing new talent. In order to change the identity of the station Ray needed up-and-coming young talent to help promote it. That's where *The Tom Green Show* came in.

From the moment he saw the pineapple on his desk, Ray was intrigued and knew he'd found the new face of cable. "Properties like *The Tom Green Show* helped to bring people back to the channel so that they could take another look, and helped to create credibility for us," boasted Ray Skaff. Over the years, a number of Letterman wanna-bes had proposed similar late-night talk shows. Ray wanted the new Rogers schedule to be different from what was already on the tube. He was looking for something out of the ordinary. He was unaware of just how bizarre Tom Green and his show really were until he sat down with the young star and his two broadcasting buddies to discuss the "pineapple proposal" at length. He was taken a little off guard when the wide-eyed young broadcasting students first burst into his office. Tom's tall, lanky frame was almost comical to Ray. He was bursting at the seams with energy and enthusiasm, and he was serious about bringing his radio show to television. He was willing to do *anything* to make it happen. The three students explained the format for the broadcast. It was a live studio show with a guest band. It would be nonstop action on the set with quirky little things going on all the time, interspersed with shocking and bizarre on-location skits.

After talking for close to an hour, Ray was very interested in taking on the program, but at the same time had some serious reservations. The show's format was fixed around three main figures: Tom Green, Darcy De Toni, and Trevor Cavanagh. All were second-year students at Algonquin College finishing up their broadcasting diplomas. Alarm bells went off in Ray's head as he talked with the young team. How much attention would these young students be able to give this program? He figured their focus would be divided between school, chores, girlfriends, and partying, and they might lose their enthusiasm for the show. "We weren't sure if it would work," said Ray, thinking back to the day he sat down with the trio. "Producing any TV show is very time-consuming. You have to look at the balance between time invested and the final product. We weren't entirely sure they were committed to doing it."

Putting their concerns aside, Ray and Karen pitched the idea to a room full of the station's producers and production staff at Rogers' annual planning session. They dissected the show, measuring the positive against the negative, and wound up deciding to give the group a shot. "We all agreed that it was a different concept and it was going to be funny," said Ray, whose feelings were seconded by Karen. "Being the community station we were able to throw caution to the wind and take on the show." At that time Rogers was winding up production on another comedy program, *Don't Watch This*, and was looking for something funny to replace it with. The consensus was to take a limited gamble on the show. In July of 1994, Ray offered *The Tom Green Show* a four- to six-

Monkey in the middle: Tom surrounded by his original crew (1995)
COURTESY ROGERS COMMUNITY TELEVISION

show series debuting in September. It would give the group enough room to develop their idea without making Rogers commit to an entire season. The agreement was advantageous to everyone involved.

Although Ray and the Rogers production staff were a little skeptical about the amount of time Tom, Darcy, and Trevor could give to organizing the hour-long broadcast each week, they couldn't help but admire their determination. What happened over the course of the following four weeks was enough to amaze and shock Ray. He was astounded by the range of their talents and willingness to give up the majority of their spare time in support of the show, and he was certain that their scholastic efforts were falling a distant second behind their passion for *The Tom Green Show*.

In four short weeks, the program found its stride. The strong creative energy around the show grabbed the attention of TV viewers who innocently switched to Rogers Community 22. It wasn't only the audiences that fell under *The Tom Green Show* spell, however; it was also staff and volunteers at Rogers. Every week the show went to air in the St. Laurent studios, a small army of broadcasting students and wanna-bes gathered to help make it happen. "It was truly incredible," said Karen, who would venture into the studios every Thursday evening for the live broadcast. "There would be flocks of high school kids lining up to watch the show and they started bringing their parents. It was a great thing to watch because Tom was a role model for the kids and the show offered them a safe environment to hang out."

Just a few short weeks after taking a chance on the bizarre college student, Ray found himself once again calling Tom into his office for a talk. The difference was that this time he wanted to renew the show for the upcoming season. Tom Green had created a buzz around town and Ray loved the feel of it. "There were days when I would watch the show and cringe," Ray confessed. "I would leave a stream of voice mails for everyone involved, but the majority of days I would just sit there and laugh."

During the premiere season, as the show began to develop its main focus, Ray was witness to the cult following that was developing around town. He found out quickly that viewers either loved Tom enthusiastically or they hated his guts. There was no in-between. "Tom is amazing — he'll do just about anything," one soaked audience member said after Tom sprayed him with a hose during a studio taping. "He's friggin' nuts!" "Tom is so awesome. He's the funniest person in the world," one fan called in to the Rogers viewer-response line. "Tom Green's just a riot. He's a really rockin' dude." The response line was jammed with calls from teenage fans pleading that Tom come emcee their high school graduations or talent nights.

The first season on Rogers, in 1994, *The Tom Green Show* was fairly tame. There was no human excrement or cell phones being inserted into dead animal carcasses. The content restrictions were monitored by full-time Rogers producer Ray Hagel, assigned by Ray Skaff to the show as a way of keeping the series in line with the station's philosophy. "We gave Ray some parameters," Ray Skaff said. "He was there to be the police and their conscience." Even with the security blanket of having a staff member at the studio, Ray sometimes still found it hard to sleep at night. As Tom developed more of a following, the risks he was taking increased and the craziness of the stunts escalated. Tom was in control

*Jason Leroux, Tom (covered in flour!),
and Ray Skaff in the Rogers lobby*

of the show and would change its course in a split second. Ray found himself praying every time he turned on the television or sat in the studio audience during a taping. "I never knew what was going to happen, but I did know from week to week it was always going to be something different," confessed Ray Skaff. "I always just said, 'Oh, God, please be sure this doesn't come back to haunt me.'"

✳

Strapping a pile of raw meat to his head, Tom walked up and down the streets of the trendy Byward Market in Ottawa talking with unsuspecting shoppers about anything he could think of. With blood from the raw meat dripping down his face, Tom tried to engage passers-by in conversation. Most people didn't know what to make of the lunacy, and the fact that he didn't even acknowledge the meat fastened to his head made the joke even funnier. "For the most part people thought he was making a political statement of some sort," said Darcy De Toni. "That's what happens when you're only a block from the Parliament buildings." The meat segment was slated to be used for the first episode, in September of 1994.

Feelings of anxiety and fear overtook Darcy, Trevor, and Tom the night before the first taping. Worries bombarded them: Would all the guests show up? Would the band be there and ready for their cue? Would the studio audience think Tom was funny? They really didn't know what to expect, but wanted to be prepared for anything. The street segments were edited and in the can, with some to spare in case a guest didn't appear. They would arrive early at the St. Laurent studios to set up the stage and lighting, and they had enlisted some of their chums from the broadcasting course to help create a familiar atmosphere backstage. Tom's dreams of walking in the footsteps of his idol, David Letterman, were about to be realized. It was show time.

Bounding out onto the stage, Tom took up his role as the show's host and easily made the transition from radio DJ to comic personality. For his part, Glenn easily adopted his role as the lovable sidekick — someone viewers could relate to and measure the mayhem against. "The pretense was that he symbolized 'everyman,'" said Trevor. "He was a good foil for the craziness." In fact he became so entrenched in his character that eventually the guys would film and edit their street segments and show them to Glenn for his approval. "He was used as a measure to decide whether a segment would be funny or not," said Trevor.

The next hour of live television, the inaugural episode of *The Tom Green Show*, left the crew with little to do. With only two guests scheduled for the program, each was on the stage for upwards of 10 minutes, which translated into interviews that dragged on and on. It was a slow-moving pace that was matched by a listlessness from the crowd. The show perked up, however, every time Tom cut to his man-on-the-street segments; they brought the audience to life and mocked conventional humor. Whatever surface problems existed with the flow of the show, one thing was certain — they were embarking on a new kind of talk show with an innovative approach and comical irreverence, and the reaction from viewers was instantaneous and affirming. Positive feedback poured in on the Rogers viewer-response line awarding kudos to Tom for being brave enough to act out what others could only imagine. It was the start of something big.

✱

While most adults were horrified by the insane antics of the host of *The Tom Green Show* — such as when he walked out into a farmer's field and began licking the cows' salt block — the weird humor did not put off TV and radio personality Ken Rockburn. At the time Ken was hosting the half-hour television program *Rockburn and Company* on the mighty CBC, where he profiled people in the arts. It was after 11 p.m. one Thursday evening that Ken, suffering from a bout of insomnia, was flipping through the dial looking for something to watch. After an endless stream of news programs and infomercials he tuned in to Rogers Cable 22. He was caught a bit off guard by what he saw on the community channel.

"It was so completely bizarre and really interesting, so I watched," said Rockburn. "I think Tom was on the roof of a building doing karate kicks and I thought, 'This is not average fare for the cable station.'" The crazy antics of the rooftop rebel gave Ken an idea for a *Rockburn and Company* profile. Picking up the phone he dialed his producer's home number and asked her to tune in to Rogers. "We should get this guy for the show," he told her. "He would make a very interesting guest." It was Tom's first big break in TV. *Rockburn and Company* contacted the station and asked for an interview with Tom and permission to tape a behind-the-scenes segment of *The Tom Green Show* to air on CBC. With only three shows to its credit, *The Tom Green Show* was quickly becoming a hot property.

"We were all so excited," said Darcy. "It seemed to be happening overnight — we were getting recognition for our little volunteer program. It was fantastic." The crew from *Rockburn and Company* appeared the following week to watch and record the taping of a street segment. On a bustling Ottawa street, Tom, equipped with a roll of the ever-powerful duct tape and a smile, climbed some eight feet up in the air and taped himself to a light pole. As shoppers and businesspeople crossed the street, Tom shouted down from his perch, "Do you know what time it is?" or "Could I get some change?"

The Rockburn crew stood a safe distance away and filmed the entire stunt, getting huge laughs at the weird looks Tom was receiving from passers-by. Ken got a close-up perspective of the spectacle from the adjacent street corner. He kept incognito by leaning on the lamppost reading a newspaper, listening to how people responded to the weirdo hanging up above them. For the remainder of their footage, the crew ventured into the St. Laurent studio and listened in on the story meetings, shot the behind-the-scenes preparation, and filmed the studio segments of *The Tom Green Show*. It was an almost surreal experience for Rockburn. "It was done on so many different levels," Rockburn said, recalling the interview fondly. "We were taping the watching of a show being taped." For the studio intro Ken appeared as Tom's guest and was drawn in by the wackiness of the show. "You got the feeling behind the scenes that they put a lot of effort into the preparation of the show but once they were on the air everyone adapted to Tom," said Ken.

The spontaneous nature of the show was irresistible and Rockburn couldn't help but get caught up in it. Before his studio piece, Ken was informed by one of his producers that during the interview a guy in a shower cap and robe would appear in the window behind Tom's desk and start ranting about how bad his shower was. This gave Ken an idea.

Thinking it was to be an impromptu sketch, he was eager to participate and add a little joke of his own. He thought it would be hilarious if, when the guy started ranting about his poor shower, Ken would toss him a bar of soap. When the segment started and the shower guy came out onto the stage rambling, Ken threw the soap at him to help solve his shower dilemma. Ken caught the shower guy completely by surprise and thought it was pretty funny how he stood there looking puzzled and dumbfounded. What he didn't know was that the shower-guy sketch was planned in advance and when Ken added the soap it sent the prepared skit down the drain.

"My impression was that it was ad-libbed, but it wasn't," confessed Ken. "Me throwing him the soap completely screwed up the rest of his ranting." By adding the new prop to the shower skit, however, Ken contributed to the underlying format of the show without even knowing it. "What I realized later is that *The Tom Green Show* is planned to a point and then it's anarchy. It's very clever."

The Rockburn interview gave *The Tom Green Show* a certain credibility that could be used to market the program. However, having only one paid staff member meant that Darcy, Trevor, and Tom had to do all their own publicity if they wanted media coverage. They found themselves cold-calling *all* of the media outlets in town, exhausting every possibility in print, radio, and television. The *Rockburn and Company* exposure had given them a taste of success and they were hungry for more. But not all media outlets were so receptive to this new style of comedy — they were given the cold shoulder by one TV station that thought they were too "inexperienced" to warrant real attention and by another that said they should be airing their program on Saturday mornings for younger audiences. The rejections were frustrating for the young television crew. They knew that they had a marketable product if they could grab the attention of a seasoned reporter, yet it seemed they were headed in the wrong direction.

✳

Standing on the top diving platform at the Carleton University pool, Tom looked down at the chanting swarm of his young admirers outfitted in swim trunks and bathing caps. He couldn't help laughing. Here he was dressed in full hockey gear and about to dive off the high board. "Tom! Tom! Tom!" the children egged him on from below. Overcome by a burst of courage, he sprang off the board and plunged into the sparkling waters below.

Fans were mesmerized by the lengths their fearless hero would go to make them laugh. His humor was infectious, and catching on fast, as the audience tuned in each week to see what insane stunt Tom would perform next. Parents began to wonder just what hold this untamable jokester had over their children and why. That's exactly what caused CBC affiliate CBOT's station manager, Allan Pressman, to tune in for the first time. He wondered what the show his son was so crazy for was all about. "My son was a religious follower of Tom's and I would tune in from time to time," admitted Allan. "What I saw was comedy and uniqueness on a limited budget. Tom Green had great potential." So much so that Allan decided to bring Tom and group in for a meeting. He was considering bringing *The Tom Green Show* to the CBC, but he'd have to sit down with the young production team and discuss the possibilities of developing a pilot episode.

Pressman asked the group to come up with a bible for the show, describing all of its contents and direction. This was a project Tom, Darcy, and Trevor had been scripting since the first episode and they were thrilled to meet with Pressman. Allan was impressed by the range of talent and creativity demonstrated by the small group as he sat and listened while they pitched him dozens of ideas they'd developed for the show. They showed promise, he had to admit, but he was leery of giving a network show to three young men still finishing up their broadcasting degrees. He needed more certainty. That's when Tom piped in that he could enlist the help of Chris Mullington, a well-known Ottawa producer with a proven track record in making cutting-edge material. Mullington had worked with Tom on a piece for the CBC show *Life: The Program*. Chris had been working on a piece about up-and-coming garage bands and Tom's group Organized Rhyme was recommended to him. "We followed the group around for an entire day. It was a riot," said Mullington.

With Chris on board, Allan was willing to let *The Tom Green Show* have its shot. Along with a small infusion of money, the little cable show from Ottawa was given the opportunity to develop a pilot to be aired on the CBC network. The group was caught in a whirlwind of activity. Everything was happening very quickly. They'd been granted a network pilot even before the final episode of the first season had aired. They were well on their way, but they had a lot of work — and some rough roads — ahead of them.

✳

Designing the pilot took up most of the summer of 1995. On top of regular story and production meetings, the crew had to plan and film a new opening sequence and several field segments for approval by the CBC. For Chris and Tom this meant making a few compromises so that the show would be acceptable to a wider audience. One field segment in which Tom was walking along the side of a highway with a sign reading "Cocaine for sale" was nixed due to content. The more vulgar and socially irresponsible the piece, the more quickly it was rejected from the lineup. Tensions were beginning to run high as Tom began to feel that the CBC was trying to dictate the content of the pilot.

"Chris was in one corner saying we had to conform a little for the pilot and then once we got a show we could expand the boundaries," said Darcy of the tumultuous times. "But Tom didn't want to sell out to the CBC. And they wanted more structure than we had on Rogers." In the end Chris and Tom clashed over creative differences and parted ways amicably before the pilot was completed. Once Chris was off the project, however, the contract was broken with the CBC. It was one of the most depressing blows *The Tom Green Show* had suffered during their short introduction to television. On the upside, they had little time to mourn the dismantling of the CBC deal because production for their second season on Rogers got underway in mid-August. They had planned to kick off the season with a live show from the Ex, an annual fair in Ottawa's Lansdowne Park.

Setting their frustrations aside, the crew redirected their focus on producing the Ex show. They invited radio personality Lowell Green and CJOH news director Max Keeping to be guests on the program. They set up a stage at the back of one of the buildings on the park and seating was arranged for approximately 200 people. What happened next surprised everyone involved with the show.

Close to 400 fans packed into the arena to watch the live version of *The Tom Green Show*. "It turned out better than we could have ever anticipated," remarked Darcy. "Tom was really in his element taking in the energy of the crowd." The show started off with Glenn and Tom drawing a portrait of Lowell. "It was funny because we all knew Lowell's voice from the radio but no one really knew what he looked like. It was a great gag," said Darcy. "Glenn's picture was really close to real life while Tom's was way off!"

The Ex show was a huge success, both creatively and for exposing the show to a larger potential audience. The disappointment that came with the crumbling of the CBC pilot was overshadowed by the positive reaction of fans to the new season on Rogers. And with that success came doubts. They soon realized they had a lot on their plates with filming, editing, writing, and marketing their show. For Tom, Trevor, and Darcy the focus began to shift as their attentions were being pulled in many different directions. The challenge now was to keep it all together.

4

GREEN AND BEAR IT

Sitting in her office at Lacewood Productions, an Ottawa animation studio, Merilyn Read found her attention wandering to a file folder on her desk. It was filled with newspaper clippings of a virtually unknown TV host — Tom Green. His name had popped up a few times in the industry and she was impressed by the amount of media attention focused on this kid who hosted a volunteer show for the community cable station. But she already had enough on her plate. As the head of development at Lacewood at the time, Merilyn was up to her neck in proposals, production schedules, and sponsorship agreements — something she had grown accustomed to since forming her own company, MTR Entertainment, in 1983.

One of MTR's first productions had come about unexpectedly. On a hunch she flew to Paris to speak with children's author Laurent de Brunhoff. Merilyn was hoping to convince the writer to sell her the television rights for the tale "Babar and Father Christmas." Not only did she succeed in garnering the TV rights, but she also produced the animated program to critical acclaim. In 1987, she, with fellow producer Alison Clayton, won a Gemini Award for Best Animated Programme or Series. With that success under her belt Merilyn went to work for Lacewood as head of development. Her time there was important for two major reasons. The first was the number of high-profile projects she worked on, including two prime-time specials for The Disney Channel. The second, and most important, is that it was there that she met Tom Green.

Producing has a reputation for being a job with overwhelming responsibility. It demands exceptional organization and communication skills, along with the ability to foresee the goals of the production company's investment. Merilyn is a perfect fit for the job. She is comfortable in high-pressure situations and thrives on the energy they create. She excels when it comes to reading people and figuring out what makes them tick. This is an asset she acquired while working as a journalist and further honed as a producer.

Tom Green was a compelling figure, but she had plenty of other work to attend to and pushed him from her mind. That is, until one of the animators she was working with on a project at Lacewood Productions brought his name back to her attention. "You see, I have this friend, Tom Green," he said to Merilyn in a matter-of-fact tone. "He's getting really frustrated 'cause he had a pilot for the CBC but it didn't work out." She was intrigued by the plight of this budding comic. "Why don't you tell your friend to come in and see me?" she offered. "There's no harm in seeing what he's got."

True to her word, a few weeks later, Merilyn agreed to see Tom. His reputation had preceded him — her friends and colleagues warned her to be ready for anything. This guy was nuts! This was the person who

Merilyn Read with her pride and joy on the set of the CBS pilot
PHOTO BY FRED CHARTRAND

thought strapping French bread to his head and dancing around town was normal. Whatever she'd been told in advance, nothing could have prepared her for her first meeting with Tom. Instead of bounding into her office and baiting her with some comedic phrase or crazy stunt, he walked in with a sullen look on his face and quietly took a seat across the desk from her.

"He was kind of a downer," she recalled of the meeting with a chuckle. "He was this tall, lanky, skinny person who sat down and was kind of depressed." He explained with all sincerity how he had worked the summer before on a pilot for the CBC but had parted ways with his producer because they didn't share the same sense of humor. "He was tired of working for Rogers for free and wanted to go to the next level," said Merilyn. "He said he had to do it soon or his parents were basically going to tell him to get a real job." He slid a pile of papers across the desk for her to look at. As she read them, she was immediately impressed. They contained a proposal for the show with each element carefully broken down and explained. She realized this depressed kid sitting in her office with a dismal look on his face was serious about this show and her maternal instincts kicked in. She felt an urge to help him achieve his goals. "I guess you better show me a tape of *The Tom Green Show*," she said forcefully. "If I'm going to call some of my contacts at the CBC to try and get the deal back on track I should know what I'm working with."

A few days later Merilyn sat down and watched a highlight reel of *Tom Green* footage that had previously aired on Rogers. She was delighted by what she saw on the screen. It was raw and creative, and although there were many pieces that weren't all that funny, she recognized that it had enormous potential. She knew he had a show that would appeal to Gen-Xers. Now all she had to do was get it to a network. She picked up the phone and put the wheels in motion. The first call she made was to resign from her position at Lacewood in 1996. It was time for her to redirect her focus to MTR, and she had a feeling *The Tom Green Show* just might be the defining program she was looking for.

✱

When you are working so closely on a project it's sometimes hard to differentiate between your own objectives and the ones for the show. That's exactly what happened to the crew of *The Tom Green Show* during the two years on Rogers. As the show progressed, it sucked both viewers and crew into its demented world of comedy — no one was immune, as Merilyn quickly discovered when she came on board. "I was fast realizing that the people that I would normally find really smelly on street corners with their caps out were revered guests on our show," she said with a laugh. "I began to look at street people differently." She confessed to developing a thick skin and even checking out their smells to help her decide if they would be good guests. Her newly developed penchant for rancid smells led her on some very outrageous quests. "There would be times when I would be driving along and I'd look at roadkill and think, 'God, that's a nice piece of roadkill. I wonder if I could stop? I wonder if I could pull over and pick it up?'" The world began to take on a whole new warped appearance.

Evidence of this change in philosophy was always present backstage at the studio tapings as an eclectic group of performers, street people, and eccentric individuals gathered to share their stories on camera with Tom. Guests included characters like Tom Dean, an ocularist who designed realistic artificial eyeballs, and "Hugo the French Guy," an Algonquin College student whose lifelong ambition was to be the star of a porno movie. "He loved women and would come on after his travels and talk about the differences between women around the globe," remarked Darcy De Toni. Each week new characters would appear — people Tom had met on the street while filming his segments and who he thought would make great interviews.

This style of booking guests sometimes created very explosive situations that had to be defused by guest coordinator Danielle Lacelle. As a guest liaison Danielle had one of the most difficult positions on the show. It was her task to ensure that the guests were kept unaware that they were about to be part of a comedy program. Most thought they were guests on a talk show where they would be able to showcase their talents or advertise products from cement to razor blades. With guests walking out onto the stage totally unaware of what was in store for them, Tom had the upper hand when it came to the interviews.

For one segment, a chef came out thinking he was there to prepare a dish of mussels but, in fact he was in for a rude awakening. He was greeted by Tom swinging a huge baseball bat at the stove, destroying the mussels, and the saucepan — and the chef's dignity in the mix. This being live television, all the chef could do was stand there looking into the camera with a fake smile on his face, waiting anxiously for the humiliation to stop. In another clip, Tom had invited a dominatrix named Cintra to be a guest after meeting her the evening before in a nightclub. Chatting with her he had discovered that one of her many talents was to pee on people for a nominal fee. Finding this fascinating, he asked Cintra onto the show to discuss her career. Dressed in a shiny black latex-like outfit and wearing a heavy coat of makeup, Cintra came out onstage and was seriously interviewed by Tom, who found her skills impressive. "You actually pee on people?" he questioned before asking her to demonstrate her abilities for the audience. He tried, unsuccessfully, to coax her into peeing into a pot that was shielded behind a curtain. She denied his request, and looked like she was more than a little uncomfortable.

Discomfort was the reaction experienced by most guests when they realized *The Tom Green Show* was not just a talk show but a late-night comedy program. "Sometimes he would use people on an item that they hadn't given their permission for," Merilyn said with a laugh. "Very often he would use people without getting their permission and so we'd end up, during a studio taping, with people coming up to us saying, 'We're not here to see the show, we're here to sue!'" Guests who were startled to find out they were part of a comedy show rather than a serious program were, more often than not, outraged at the duping. "We once had a guest who was fine during the taping of the show, but then she returned with her husband and said if we used that piece they'd definitely sue."

If there was one thing that was for certain, *The Tom Green Show* was anything but dull — keeping the format a secret from the guests helped to generate a mysterious intensity behind the scenes.

✳

To compose and maintain the unpredictable nature of the show, Tom was always on the lookout for outrageous elements to add. For the most part he enlisted the help of his good friends. During the second phase of the show, Tom's buddy Derek Harvie, who was completing his film and English degree at the University of Toronto, joined the cast as a correspondent. Soon Tom began reading a "Letter from Derek" each week. The author would take everyday matters and give his twisted opinion on them. The segments became so popular that they were quickly embedded in the show's format. After Derek completed his degree in Toronto he moved back into his parents' home in Ottawa and started volunteering as a full-time writer for *The Tom Green Show* — much to the chagrin of his parents, who were hoping he would start his career with a paying job after completing university.

Having Derek on board gave Tom the confidence and energy to try even more outrageous stunts. Derek's mind was even more twisted than Tom's and he would often go the distance for each of his jokes, actually putting himself in physical danger just to get the laugh. Derek's input as a writer gave Tom more time to focus on his comedy rather than having to create all the concepts and write the scripts. As an added bonus, Tom and Derek had been friends since Grade 3 at Robert Hopkins. They were compatible as friends and as a comedy team. After all, they shared the same distorted sense of humor. "They would go off on these weird little trips together," Merilyn recalled. On one such trip the comedy duo ventured off on a camping excursion in the Gatineau Hills with nothing but the clothes on their backs. "They didn't take any food on purpose because then it meant they had to kill something, cook it, and eat it," Merilyn said affectionately. "They'd take themselves into weird experiences together." The pair saw the open road as their muse and always returned from their adventures with plenty of new story ideas.

It wasn't only the trips that fascinated the comedy duo — it was people's bizarre behavior that captured their attention. That was the main reason they went on a road trip to St. Catharines, Ontario, during the 1995 trial of convicted sex-killer Paul Bernardo, who was charged with the gruesome rape and murder of two teenage girls, Kristen French and Leslie Mahaffy. The dark details of the trial captivated both Derek and Tom so much that the two drove the five and a half hours to

Tom with Derek Harvie
PHOTO BY DOUGLAS WALKER

St. Catharines to get a close-up view of the home where Bernardo had lived with his former wife, Karla Homolka. "They went up to the home where Bernardo lived and they sat on the front steps and just started talking about it and imagining it," Merilyn said. They filmed segments for the show, and the following day the pair showed up in the courtroom to take the place of absent journalists in order to listen to the history-making trial and gain an insider's perspective. "They had such a fascination, not with the horribleness of [the case] but a fascination with people's behaviors," Merilyn said.

Merilyn shared Tom and Derek's interest in human behavior. One of the reasons she had decided to produce *The Tom Green Show* was that she was so beguiled with their personalities. She found it amazing how completely different Tom could be when discussing work. When it came to the show he was a tough cookie who would not compromise his integrity or vision at any cost, but before a live taping he was a nervous wreck. In fact Tom would stop eating a few days before the tapings and stress would cause him to lose his voice come show time.

As soon as Merilyn and Danielle discovered this, they tried to remedy the situation. When it came time to roll the cameras, backstage would look like the kitchen in a nursing home. Piles of boxes of chilled bottled water and cases of Ensure, a nutrient-replacement beverage, would line the small dressing area. Because he was skinny and tall to begin with, it was always readily apparent when Tom was suffering from his bouts of stress. "I remember one time when he had his shirt off and I went into his dressing room," Merilyn said, making a face to illustrate how she felt. "And I said, 'What the hell is going on? You're pathetic.'" Looking at his sickly, bony body, she ordered him, with a laugh, to immediately put his shirt back on because "he was gonna make me gag."

Backstage there was always something going on, whether it was panic attacks or screaming guests threatening to sue. It sometimes seemed that the show that went to air was tamer than what was happening behind the curtain.

✱

Dressed in a pristine white lab coat and carrying a small clipboard, Tom marched into a grocery store and up to the checkout clerk. "Have you heard of any illness or death caused as a result of people ingesting the mustard?" he seriously asked the clerk before walking down one of the aisles. "You don't want to buy bad mustard," Tom said, pulling the lid off a squeezable container of mustard and pouring the yellow substance down his throat. The skit was one of the first filmed for the CBC pilot.

As the show's producer, Merilyn had successfully negotiated the same deal for the pilot as *The Tom Green Show* had secured a year earlier. They were given $5,000 and some of the best equipment and personnel CBC had to offer to see what they could come up with. Merilyn was satisfied with the small chunk of money they'd offered her to start production on the pilot but she was determined to raise more cash through sponsorship. There was no way they could get the pilot finished with $5,000. A few weeks later she reported back to the crew that they had two major sponsors hooked up with the show: Panasonic donated some equipment and Molson came on board with financial support and the occasional supply of beer. Things were looking up.

By the end of the summer the segments were shot, and all that remained was the taping of the in-studio segment. Both Merilyn and Tom wanted to make a big impact and reach as many viewers as possible. For this they decided to enlist some star power. Merilyn contacted the agent for comedian Joe Flaherty, formerly of *sctv*, and confirmed a guest appearance for the pilot. The production crew met daily to come up with different story lines for the pilot. They needed a new layer to draw the attention of the audience.

Tom and Derek decided to introduce a mascot for the group — a hairless albino guinea pig. The idea was to cover Tom's desk with a layer of plush grass and harness the animal to a pole in the middle. During the show, Skinny, as the pig was affectionately nicknamed, would roam around the table without Tom ever acknowledging his existence. So off Merilyn and Derek went to find the rare guinea pig. Their search ended at a pet store where one of the hideous-looking animals was kept in a cage in the backroom. "They were afraid because it was so sensitive. If

The famous turf-covered desk
PHOTO BY FRED CHARTRAND

it was brought into the pet store with the other animals it might die," said Merilyn. Deciding to give it a loving home, she forked over the $75 for the weird-looking animal and Derek vowed to give it a good, stable home so it would feel safe.

Derek adopted the small creature and took it home to introduce to his large German shepherd. It took only a short time for the enormous pooch and the skittish pig to forge a bond. The dog would carry Skinny around in its mouth or the pig would scurry along behind while the dog went for a run outside. They were steadfast friends — so much so that when it came time to tape the pilot Skinny felt lost without his doggy pal.

The turf-covered desk was rigged with a leash and harness, and Skinny was brought onto the stage. "As soon as we put it on the desk in its little harness it went bloody berserk," said Merilyn, reenacting the comical episode with her own body. "It ran round and round in concentric circles so quickly that it freaked." The skittish animal was released from its harness and taken backstage, giving it a chance to relax. Not knowing what to do with the pig, they offered it a snack and some encouraging words before trying to put it back on the desk again. "It did the exact same thing and all I kept thinking was, 'This animal is going to hang itself on national TV and the animal rights people are going to come after us.'"

The guinea pig was banished from the pilot and returned to Derek's home to play with its canine buddy. The group realized that Skinny needed to feel secure in its environment, so they designed a prop desk that was covered with such delicious treats and treasures that the pig would feel it had died and gone to heaven. Their plan worked — almost too well. Once the pig uncovered the delicacies in its new stomping grounds — popcorn, lettuce, carrots, and a wide assortment of veggies — it started looking forward to show time. "We'd put it on the desk and he ruled," said Merilyn. "There were times when the audience would sit there and watch this little pig eat his way through an entire show. He ruled!"

Even though Skinny was a no-go for the CBC pilot, Tom seemed unfazed. They already had an abundance of animals for the show. Earlier on they had filmed a touching barnyard greeting for his parents by turning their home into a petting zoo, where the smell of excrement was so strong they had to air out the house for two weeks after the stunt. Also added to the show was a much-loved celebrity-watching segment where Tom finds look-alikes for famous Hollywood types. Completing the half-hour was a musical interlude by Ottawa band Punchbuggy and a piece in which Tom forged a friendship with a man he met on the street and nicknamed "Dan the Man." He convinced the friendly gentleman to participate in a pantomime routine where the pair wrapped themselves in plastic sheets and frolicked around, pretending to be amoebas. Working out all the kinks in the editing suites, Tom and Merilyn were both pleased with the final result. They agreed the footage was unconventional, but tame enough to be acceptable to the bureaucratic machine of the CBC.

As Merilyn worked closely with the development of *The Tom Green Show* she began to notice more and more that her frame of mind was expanding. They were successfully conditioning her to appreciate their humor. One Friday afternoon, for instance, Merilyn was distracted by a phone call. She heard a familiar voice on the other end of the line. "Do you want to go see *The Truman Show* with Jim Carrey? Can you come? Can you come tonight?" Tom's voice bubbled over with energy. It was one of the very special memories she has of working with Tom — in order to test out her reaction to comedy without coming right out and asking her, he would invite her to movies he found especially funny and see how they affected her. Instead of watching the movie, which he'd already seen, he would sit in the chair beside her and study her responses.

"It was a strange experience because he'd always be moving his head around," she said, mimicking his movement. "It was like he had a nervous tic or something." So the two made plans for a "movie review" and Tom picked her up outside her office. "It was funny because he picked me up in his brand-new green Jeep and he was so proud," she said. The pair set off for the theater only to find out it was the opening night of *The Truman Show* and there was a lineup down the front steps of the multiplex to get tickets. As the two walked up to the theater doors, Tom's fans in the crowd recognized their hero. "Everyone that age knew Tom by that point and we were told by the crowd that the movie was already sold out for the evening." About to turn around and head back to the car, Merilyn felt a tug at the sleeve of her coat. "OK,

Glenn, Dan the Man, Tom, and Ray get ready for a skit
PHOTO BY FRED CHARTRAND

let's go," Tom whispered in her ear. "Just follow me inside." Not knowing exactly what was happening, she followed along behind Tom as he walked up to the rope barricading the theater corridor. "Just do what I tell you," he said in a muffled tone as he lifted up the velvet rope barrier. "OK, just duck, now duck again," he gave her directions while he put the rope back into place. The two escaped from the main entrance down a long, dark corridor and Merilyn, her eyes adjusting to the dim lighting, realized they'd just snuck into the movie theater. "We walked into the theater and we were the only ones there, so I said to Tom, 'This is some irony that we're seeing *The Truman Show* and we haven't paid for it," she laughed, thinking back to the occasion. "I said to him, 'This is really good, Tom, OK, now I want you to go out and get our free popcorn!" She realized then and there that not only was he having an effect on her comedic senses but also on her personality. "He was turning a middle-aged producer into a total delinquent," she confessed. "And I loved every minute of it."

✱

Pacing backstage at the studios of the CBC Ottawa affiliate, CBOT, Merilyn was more than a little nervous. It was only a few hours before the taping of the studio segment for the pilot and she was growing frustrated. She'd already had countless discussions with Tom about the composition of the show. In particular, she questioned Glenn's abilities as cohost. "I thought Glenn was so unfunny," she remarked with authority. "I said to Tom, 'You are going to have to get rid of him if we're going to work together because he's just a big lump. I can't work with him.'" Tom had always ignored her threats, giving her lectures about their bond of friendship and his undeniable ability to play the straight man to outrageous comedy. Whenever she spoke with him about "the Glenn situation" he would do a little routine she fondly nicknamed "looping." "There was a very strong male team here. They were headstrong and very sure they were right in everything they did, and who gave a damn anyway," said Merilyn. So to get a point across, especially as the only woman, she would have to do it in a very strong way. "When Tom would not let go of a point, he'd keep on and on about it," she recalled. "It was like a concentration camp experience, until you finally caved in."

She sometimes found it easier to let them win the small battles, so she agreed to give Glenn another chance, but she still felt uneasy — so much so that before the taping at CBOT she took Glenn out to the parking lot to confront him on the issue. Getting straight to the point, she told him in no uncertain terms that he was going to have to be funnier. She explained to him that in order for him to be a good cohost he was going to have to carry some lines and react to what was happening on set. "I was pretty serious about this one and I said to Tom, 'Unless this guy improves he's off!'" For the first time in her history with the show, she put her foot down. They were going to have to make some serious changes, or she would do it for them.

For his part, Tom kept up the "We Love Glenn" vigil and directed a little more attention towards his cohost, repeatedly explaining to Merilyn that "people love Glenn." Merilyn's reaction was a little less dramatic. "I would tell him time and time again, 'Look, I think you're seeing something in this guy that I don't think anyone in the world is seeing,'" she remarked bluntly. Their efforts paid off and Glenn soon began to open up and start interacting with Tom and the show's guests. "I saw that Glenn would go to great lengths to participate in his buddy's pranks and he would be the butt of so many jokes," said Merilyn. She couldn't help but laugh hysterically when Tom talked Glenn into dropping his pants so that he could serenade his butt, or when Glenn and Tom, in an act of pure friendship, would make each other vomit by sticking their hands down each other's throats. "And I thought, 'Good for him, he's crazy but he's doing it.'"

Once the kinks were all worked out and the material for the show put together, all that remained was to wait for their big day — the CBC debut. It only seemed fitting that the madcap mayhem of *The Tom Green Show* pilot be aired along with the witches and ghouls on Halloween night. October 31, 1996, at 11:30 p.m. the CBC pilot was unleashed on the usually reserved network. Taking over the time slot from the regular broadcast of *Cinema Canada*, which drew an average weekly audience of 83,000 viewers nationwide, *The Tom Green Show* aired across Ontario to some 80,000 viewers.

In Ottawa, Merilyn organized for a special screening of the pilot at a seedy motel in Vanier in the east end of Ottawa. It was open to fans, crew, and anyone who was in the neighborhood. As it turned out, the room was filled with drunken street vagrants, including some Tom had met on his segment shoots in the Byward Market. "It was a real hoot," said Merilyn, remembering fondly the stench of liquor and smoke that filled the room. "It was really surreal because we were living the life of the show." With positive ratings on the four stations airing the pilot in Ontario, the *Tom Green* camp was duly excited at the real possibility of claiming a network show. Now all they had to do was wait — and wait and wait.

While things were heading in a successful direction onstage for *The Tom Green Show*, some of the original members of the show were growing frustrated with its progress. They'd been working on the show for close to two years and had yet to see a real paycheck. Now in their early 20s, they were hoping to start profitable careers and settle down. When Merilyn signed on as the series producer, some of the tasks once handled by Trevor Cavanagh and Darcy De Toni became part of her domain. Trevor and Darcy were starting to feel isolated, as if they no longer fit with the direction of the show. Ultimately the core elements of the show were still their responsibility. They were expected to venture out on segment shootings where they would spend hours in coffee shops talking about what they'd shoot and then spend an hour filming it. "We'd have discussions like, 'Let's go buy bread and stick it on your head,' then we'd realize we'd done that the previous week," recalled De Toni. It was becoming more and more of a waste of time because, as Darcy said, most of the footage that was shot by the group would not be accepted for the show. It was time to make a decision. For Darcy and Trevor it was simple. They were both looking for careers as producers or directors and needed to spread their wings and prove their talents. So after the CBC pilot was completed, the original core of Tom, Trevor, and Darcy split. Tom got the show while Trevor and Darcy went on to further their own careers in television.

A few weeks after the pilot aired, some disturbing news filtered down to Merilyn from her CBC contacts that everything was in a state of

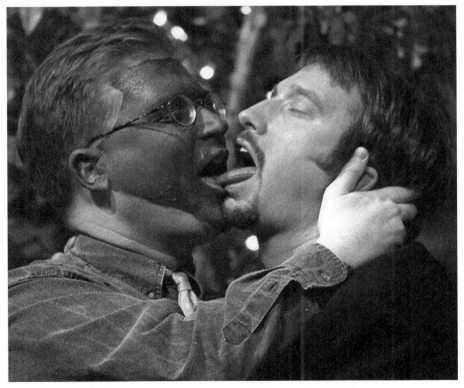

Glenn's "straight man" routine isn't always so conventional
PHOTO BY FRED CHARTRAND

limbo at the network. Among all the changes there was a new head of programming. For *The Tom Green Show* that meant the future of a network deal was once again up in the air. Something had to be done to woo the new CBC executive director of network programming. What would get Slawko Klymkiw on their side? Taking a proactive and "clean" approach to the uncertainty, Tom and company came up with a scheme to grab Klymkiw's attention. "We sent him a big box of Tide with a T-shirt and fan letter from a 50-something fan who thought Tom Green was funnier than Peter Sellers," Merilyn said jokingly. When he opened the box, the soap crystals scattered around his Toronto office, coating the floor. Inside the box Tom had packaged a tape made personally for Klymkiw saying, "Slawko Klymkiw, we LOVE YOU and we want to take you out to lunch!"

Despite Tom's "cleaner" approach to comedy and the favorable ratings, Klymkiw could not be coerced into taking a gamble on *The Tom Green Show*. "He told me he thought the show was really interesting," Merilyn said, recalling her interview with Klymkiw. "He said he couldn't tell if it was going to be sophomoric or stupid, or if it would maintain the edginess and the fun for the university crowd." For his part, Klymkiw, new to his role, wasn't looking to make any drastic changes to the CBC prime-time lineup. In terms of comedy shows they already had a full schedule for the upcoming season.

"It was wacky and irreverent and from time to time could be brilliant and smart, but it wasn't a particularly good fit for CBC prime time and we weren't investing a lot at that point in terms of late-night programming," Klymkiw said. "We didn't want to lead them on, so we released them from the commitment." For Merilyn and Tom the news was more than a letdown. It seemed like the past six months had been a rollercoaster ride of emotions: yes, they might get a network deal; no, they wouldn't; then again yes, it looked possible. In the end Klymkiw took a pass on *The Tom Green Show*, saying he wanted to keep a close eye on its development, but that he couldn't commit to support from the CBC. When he heard the news of the rejection, Tom was tremendously disappointed. It felt like the final blow. He was never going to get a network gig. Maybe it would be better if he gave in to his parents' demands and just went out and got a normal paying job. He was oblivious to the dramatic changes about to affect the television industry, but Merilyn had a feeling that one way or another *The Tom Green Show* was going to have its opportunity to shine.

5

THE GREEN LIGHT

Timing is everything when it comes to show business. That doesn't just refer to the pacing of jokes; it also pertains to the point at which you break into the industry. For Tom's television career, the timing was perfect.

In the early 1980s the CRTC (Canadian Radio-Television and Tele-communications Commission) began granting licenses to specialty channels, which by the late 1990s would have a significant impact on the television universe. With competitive programming and popular formats available for a wide range of interests, they would be successful at attracting new viewers and redirecting existing ones to the television. They would be making major waves in the industry.

It started in 1984, when MuchMusic, Tele Latino, and TSN (The Sports Network) made their debut. As the dial began to fragment with the introduction of carefully targeted specialty channels, viewers were slowly being wooed from the major networks to smaller channels. For Canadian viewers and talent this meant an opening up of the market, offering more options and a wider range of resources. By 1989 specialty channels were gaining momentum as nine more channels were added to the spectrum, including The Weather Network and YTV, a youth entertainment network.

Specialty channels were welcomed by artists who felt they offered more freedom to develop new and innovative programming. By the 1990s another slew of channels broke into the market, offering something for everyone, from the outdoor enthusiast to the budding gourmet. It was an exciting time as programming markets diversified. Audiences had more selection than ever before and Canadians had a solid training ground for their talent.

News, sports, and entertainment were heavily covered, with programming spanning intimate portraits of beloved movie stars to locker-room coverage before NHL hockey games. Only one thing was missing from the dial: a comedy outlet. The U.S. had HBO and Comedy Central, but Canadians didn't have a comedy station to develop talent on a national level. This situation was remedied in 1996 when the CRTC granted broadcasting licenses to another handful of national English-language specialty networks, including The Comedy Network.

In its successful bid for a national comedy station, The Comedy Network beat out two other competing parties whose majority shareholders surprisingly enough were Second City Television/Western International Communication Ltd. and Salter Street/CHUM Inc. The Comedy Network was awarded the license instead of the other contenders for two significant reasons: it offered the highest level of Canadian content in its proposed schedule and had dedicated a significant amount towards production of Canadian programming. The Comedy Network, with a 65% share owned by Baton Broadcasting (a majority shareholder of CTV), burst onto the market with a simple mandate: to provide a variety of comedy series, sketches, and human-interest programs 24 hours a day to a national audience. The CRTC had specified that Canadian content levels be enforced on all the stations. For The Comedy Network it meant a minimum level of 58% over the broadcast year, and not less than 72% of the evening broadcast period between 6 p.m. and midnight.

The mandatory levels of Canadian content meant that Ed Robinson, head of programming at the new channel, had his work cut out for him. Not only was he on the ground floor of setting up the operations for the network, but he also had to find the identity of the station and choose programming that would fall within the CRTC guidelines.

Trained as a chartered accountant, Ed had been introduced to the creative aspect of television production during his time at the CBC, where he had been a development and programming executive for arts, music, science, and variety shows. "It totally changed the way I thought about programming," said Ed of his time with the CBC. "I was able to gain an insight and perspective into the creative side of television." He found that his new position with The Comedy Network allowed him to further hone his creative skills — it was no longer just the bottom line and revenues the shows would generate for the network but the artistic side that mattered now.

From the CBC, it was a perfect career move to take on the role of head of programming for The Comedy Network right from the start. He knew the financial side and the importance of budgetary restraints, but he also could relate to the artistic needs of the performers. He could bring to the new network his experience from both worlds.

*

Walking into his new office at The Comedy Network in Toronto, Ed Robinson was caught off guard by the piles and piles of videotapes scattered around the room. Clearing off a spot on his desk, he glanced over a stack of proposals lying loose on the table — all desperately pitching new comedy series to the network. "Word does travel fast," he mumbled to himself while reading through the first portfolio. Distributors from the Toronto area, knowing about the startup of The Comedy Network, had worked quickly to get proposals and tapes together for Ed to peruse. "There was everything ranging from sitcoms to conventional broadcast material to really obscure and sort of out-of-control stuff," he said.

After weeks of scanning the proposals, Ed was able to get an idea of the talent that was available. But there was one thing that had to be done before purchasing any of the properties: he had to clearly define the attitude and identity of The Comedy Network. With so many comedy shows already on the dial, and the Canadian market for satirical humor dominated by *The Royal Canadian Air Farce* and *This Hour Has 22 Minutes*, Ed was in search of something different. "We didn't want to duplicate what was already available on conventional broadcasters in particular," he said. "We described the kind of attitude we wanted as irreverent, geared for adults, and untraditional in terms of the concepts." The fall schedule was split into two sections, daytime and prime time. For daytime viewing they would have to be careful about the programming they chose, taking into consideration the ages of the viewers who may be watching. It was during the prime-time hours that the network would be able to make their mark.

"Particularly after 9 p.m. broadcasters can be more adult — risk-taking and raunchy if that's what you choose," Robinson said, adding that The Comedy Network set out to offer barrier-pushing, uncensored programming that was laid out in an aggressive and bold schedule. There were so many sitcoms on the major American networks that he wasn't keen on putting any in the schedule, whether they were Canadian talent or foreign properties. He was looking to create an innovative schedule with new and dynamic programming. The closest he came to sitcoms was the purchase of *The Larry Sanders Show* and *Dream On*, which were both clearly for mature audiences because of their language and subject matter.

The second part of their mandate was the discovery and nurturing of Canadian talent. They searched for unconventional and nontraditional comedy. Setting aside the piles of tapes lying around his office, Ed ventured to a two-day conference in Ottawa for the members of the Canadian Film and Television Producers Association. The conference was filled with seminars on new productions and techniques and was organized by the Independent Producers Association. After the conference was an optional one-day session given by the Ottawa-Hull Independent Producers Association when participants were given a chance to meet with producers and talk about what new programming they might have to offer. Ed was intrigued by the conference, choosing to stay on for the third day to meet with producers and get a first-hand account of the talent available. Flipping through a number of proposals that he'd already had a chance to look at, Ed's interest was piqued. He'd already met with former stand-up comedian Greg Lawrence, who was developing the animated series *Kevin Spencer*. It was based on one of the characters in his comedy routine — a chain-smoking sociopath; it was raw, edgy, and vulgar — exactly what Ed was looking for.

Producer Merilyn Read was up against some tough competition, but she was determined to convince Robinson that he needed Tom on The Comedy Network. She put a lot of time and energy into preparing for her meeting with Ed. This was the opportunity she had been waiting for — a chance to get the show up and running across the country. Rogers had helped out considerably by putting the program on the all-Ontario Rogers and it was getting good audience response. It was time for Tom Green to be introduced to the rest of the country, and the new network was the perfect vehicle. Merilyn was growing concerned that Tom was losing his drive for the show after the CBC pilot was rejected. Despite the favorable rating it received, the CBC wasn't willing to take the gamble that it could control the show's content. Tom was growing extremely frustrated and getting a lot of pressure from his parents to give up his pipe dream and get a real paying job; Merilyn feared he was at the brink of conceding to their demands. They had already been disappointed by Tom's promising music career, which had fizzled out, and his cable show, which drew a cult following but was unable to move to the next level. The Comedy Network was her shot to make the show a success. Merilyn was bound and determined to make an impression on Ed Robinson and sell the show to The Comedy Network.

*

"This is *The Tom Green Show*. It's not *The Green Tom Show*," the opening lyrics of the program boomed from the television set as Ed watched the Ottawa comic. He was vaguely familiar with Tom Green's comedy/ talk show. He had been working for the CBC when MTR Entertainment had put together the pilot. After screening the highlight reel of the stunts Tom had performed for the Rogers version of the show, Ed's first reaction was favorable — he liked what he saw. He was intrigued by the energy and drive behind the show and captivated by the producer who sat before him. Merilyn was dynamic, energized, and stood firmly behind her belief in *The Tom Green Show*. As Ed watched Tom and his antics on the screen, Merilyn, with her strong voice and self-assured attitude, pitched the idea to him. Watching the screening tape allowed Ed to immediately see the show's potential. Tom's on-screen persona mesmerized him. He had a fresh comedic perspective and was a chaotic, multifaceted performer who would go to great lengths to entertain his fans. And Tom's program fell in line with The Comedy Network's mandate. "I thought he was wacko, really out there in terms of what he was doing," Ed said affectionately of Tom. "There was something intriguing about the way he was going against the convention of what normal comedy might be or the normal standard of what people might find to be funny."

For Ed half the fun of the show was the spontaneous reactions of its host. He felt Tom enticed people into his world by blindsiding them with his absurd, hilarious, and sometimes crude humor. Tom perfectly fit the vision Ed Robinson had for The Comedy Network. He wanted to give people something new and interesting to watch, unlike any other show they'd find on television. "It was always kind of a bit of a mystery to me as to the things that Tom chose to send up. You never knew what would be next," confessed Ed, who admits that one of his favorite stunts was when Tom painted his parents' house plaid. From the moment he saw the video footage of the couple's reaction to the unsolicited renovation, Ed was hooked. "I think he's speaking to the devil in all of us," he commented. Ed selected *The Tom Green Show* as one of the first Canadian productions on The Comedy Network. The CRTC had already granted the network a license; the only thing holding back production was reaching a deal with the cable companies and agreeing on the official launch date for the new service. Until those deals were finalized it was impossible for The Comedy Network to commit to production orders.

The next few months felt as if they were the longest Merilyn had ever endured. "It was like the summer from hell," she recalled. "Everything was in limbo. We weren't able to shoot, we weren't able to go forward." Coupled with Merilyn's concerns were Tom's parents' worries about his future. They wanted him to change his career path and get a respectable job. He was beginning to feel serious pressure from their end to get going on his career and start making some real money to support himself. "His mother literally said one Friday afternoon, 'Tom, if you don't have an income by Monday you're going to Toronto to live with your aunt and get a job!'" Being a parent herself, Merilyn could appreciate how the Greens felt about their son's future, but she was certain of one thing: he had real talent and she knew he was destined for success. It was only a matter of time. "I met him at a little coffee shop and wrote him out a check for some money to get through the next few months and it helped to relieve some of the stress," said Merilyn.

The infusion of cash helped to get Tom's creative juices flowing again. He started writing a memoir about what he was going through at the time, focusing mainly on how to pick up chicks and how to get a TV show. With time on his hands, Tom decided not to stay out of the spotlight and went back to Ottawa University's CHUO to try and get his voice back on the radio. "At that time the programming manager had a different philosophy for the station than Bob McCarthy did," explained Karen McHarg. "She didn't really like what Tom did so she wanted to take a pass on it." McHarg, a Tom Green fan from when she first met him as an intern at the station, took a stand and put him back on the air. "It's Tom Green, for God's sake, he's hilarious." The deal she'd made with the programming manager was that the show would go on probation so they could monitor its progress, and Tom was only allowed to miss hosting two shows. "I think he was really starved for the audience and wanted some attention," McHarg said candidly.

The first week Tom was scheduled to be back at the radio station some amazing things started to happen for his television show. The Comedy Network was showing real interest and wanted him to go to Toronto to meet some of the potential advertisers and bigwigs from the network. Tom was forced to miss the first CHUO broadcast, putting him in the bad books with the station manager. A few weeks later his brand of comedy would be the downfall of his radio show. For the weekly Friday broadcast he'd staged an in-depth report on prostitution with the aid of Derek and Phil. Derek, posing as a male prostitute, cruised the streets of downtown Ottawa trying to get picked up. Phil followed the intrepid reporter, giving Tom, who was in the studio, a play-by-play commentary of what was happening. "He actually got picked up and taken to an Ottawa hotel where they sort of just left the broadcast. It was like, 'Tune in next week to see what happened to Derek,'" said Karen. "We didn't really know what took place when Phil and Derek explained that it was all just a big joke for the radio." That was the last straw — the show was deemed politically incorrect and the mike was turned off. But bigger things were brewing for Tom's career in the world of TV.

In June of 1997 Ed Robinson placed a very important phone call to Merilyn Read. First he boasted about the startup of The Comedy Network slated for mid-October and then informed her that he was commissioning 13 episodes of The Tom Green Show. "Pardon?" she asked, waiting for him to repeat the news. "We've just cleared to go to air," he told her. We've agreed on a launch date for the network and I'm commissioning 13 episodes of *The Tom Green Show*." She hung up the phone, replaying the conversation over and over in her head. It was really going to happen. Things were finally looking up.

With The Comedy Network on board it meant a small budget for the crew was available, but due to the timing of the launch *The Tom Green Show* was unable to apply for further federal financing from the Canada Television and Cable Production Fund. Merilyn was creative in collecting financing for the show. She already had a lengthy agreement with Molson, a major sponsor of the CBC pilot, and she also got the idea to work with the resources previously offered to *The Tom Green Show* from its original broadcaster, Rogers Cable. She struck a deal with the community cable outlet to continue production of the show using their volunteer crews, staff workers, and equipment (close to $300,000 a year in non-monetary means). In exchange for their support, Rogers was granted the right to be the first broadcaster to air the show on their station. "We wanted to give the Ottawa viewers a chance to see Tom and we thought it was a great property and wanted to continue to support it for as many years as we could," said Ray Skaff.

It was a unique deal for everyone involved. Rogers was still affiliated with *The Tom Green Show*, Merilyn had found an innovative way of solving their financial problems, and The Comedy Network had a national program. The drought was over. The crew would go back into production for the show. There was a lot of work to be done before their spring air date. After a celebratory meeting at a local pub with Tom, Phil, Glenn, and Derek, the crew went back to work pumping out segments for The Comedy Network. Their first major decision as a network program was to take *The Tom Green Show* on the road. Like most wanna-be movie stars, Tom and company headed for the warm, sunny beaches of southern California. They went in search of sun, sand, and street fanatics for the debut of his self-titled national program.

✱

Catching people off guard creates some very unpredictable situations — exactly what Tom wanted. The only problem was that after taping for close to four years in Ottawa, his mug was getting too familiar around town. Fewer people were surprised by what he did and more often they would simply walk up to him in the middle of a stunt saying, "Hey, aren't you Tom Green?" The more people recognized him the harder it was to make the jokes real. Getting out of Ottawa, where they had been filming bits on Bank Street and Elgin Street for more than four years, offered a much-needed change of pace. Not only did it give them a break from their regular routines but it also helped with the creative process. Every day they woke up to something new and strange in their environment.

For two weeks Ray Hagel, Tom, and Derek roamed through LA and San Diego getting acquainted with the customs of each town and establishing friendly relations with the natives — relations that were sometimes a little too friendly. Tom swam with the dolphins (he was wearing a pink dress and blonde wig), cozied up to a Chilean marine officer who didn't speak English (they chatted about the similarities between the ship's apparatus and sexual acts), and got up close and personal with a number of people off the street (he would hug them while asking if they thought he was sexy). At the climax of the trip the group wound their way down to Tijuana, Mexico, to open the first ever Tom Green Land, a theme park that they hoped could compete with Disneyland. Making their way through the hot desert sand and prickly cacti, the group cordoned off a section of land and set up camp. Posting signs with pictures of the show's stars, including Derek, Phil, Glenn, Tom, and Ray, they positioned familiar props from the set on the dry land to attract wayward tourists. Tom boasted that fans would remember the George Bush mask, the NASA helmet (the same one Glenn wore with his thermal underwear on the Gravitron ride at an amusement park for astronaut training), and the ratty old blue spray-painted plaid jacket Tom had worn during some of the skits. If all those attractions didn't draw the big crowds, he suggested they scream at potential patrons, "C'mon down, it sucks!"

After spending two weeks filming on the road, the group was ready to get back home to Ottawa and, more importantly, back to work. Tom and

Ray spent the better part of five months in the editing suites at General Assembly Production Center and Rogers to put the California man-on-the-street segments together. Tom had learned the tools for editing at Algonquin College and honed them during his volunteer work at Rogers. It looked like everything was coming together; Tom was really beginning to develop a look for the show.

When The Comedy Network purchased *The Tom Green Show,* two significant changes were made. Both were complementary to the program and meant some small adjustments to the production. The first was the taping location. To give the crew more space and an audience-friendly studio environment, the set was moved to the Arts Court in Ottawa. The theater was spacious and could accommodate a larger audience. More importantly, the set could remain intact on location rather than having to be torn down after each taping. The second change had a bigger impact. The format of the show was switched from a live hour-long broadcast to a half-hour pretaped program. Although the format remained the same — studio segments intertwined with street footage and musical interludes from a guest band — the show had more of an edge. Instead of being forced to air 90% of their taped segments to fill the hour time slot, they could now be more selective in choosing what material they used. It was a relief for the crew. They finally had the opportunity to really work on the consistency of the show and develop stronger story lines.

Although Tom was supportive of the changes, he was noticeably nervous. On the cusp of national exposure, Tom was suffering from stage fright. No longer was it just Tom fooling around with the video cameras trying to entertain his buddies. Heading into the studio taping sessions meant a young and hip live audience to entertain. They would be the final judge of what was and was not funny. Days before the taping, *Ottawa Sun* TV critic Tralee Pearce sat down with the harried star and he confessed his true feelings about being the center of attention. "It will escalate to the point of insanity, right up until about 10 minutes into the first show," he said, commenting that he felt as if he were having a nervous breakdown. "For the past five months, I've been in my own little vacuum inside an editing suite. Now I'll be facing 130 people with their fingers on their chins saying, 'Oh, this better be funny. . . .'"

The Tom Green Show's crew quickly learned that being associated with The Comedy Network allowed them to take more chances. During the two years the show aired there they ripped through the barriers of conventional comedy and exposed the underbelly of their demented world, all for the amusement of their adoring fans.

✳

The more raunchy, disgusting, or outrageous the stunt, the greater the reaction Tom received from the audience. He fed off their responses. As he pushed farther and farther away from mainstream comedy acts, his fans became more dedicated. They followed their comedic hero every step of the way. Pushing the limits of the show, however, also meant pushing the envelope with his producer. For her part, Merilyn was an "imagineer." She strongly believed in Tom's creative capabilities; not only could he entertain an audience and edit his own work, but she quickly found out he could also draw and write. This kid could do it all. "What I wanted most of all was to give Tom and the guys complete freedom to create," said Merilyn. "Very rarely in our office would we ever say no to an item." She was very accepting of the way his mind worked and the ideas he and Derek came up with. Ed's feelings were similar. The time slot he set for *The Tom Green Show* — 11 p.m. Friday nights — was safely after family viewing hours, so Tom was free to express himself with few restrictions. That did not, however, mean carte blanche control over what was aired. Ed kept a close watch over what direction *The Tom Green Show* took. "When we did the first 13 episodes there were a couple of things that I thought were problematic and we didn't allow everything they did to go on air," he explained. Ed also commented that he and Tom had talked at length during the first season to ensure they were both on the same wavelength. "We wanted to define the point between what was truly shocking and maybe in bad taste and where the line was of what could be shocking and fun."

As a result of their conversation, one of the studio segments was dumped from the schedule. The joke in question began with Tom and Glenn in the studio washrooms discussing how *The Tom Green Show* does not engage in poo-poo humor. To further prove their point Tom reached into one of the washroom stalls and grabbed a piece of doo-doo from the toilet with his bare hands. He walked out into the studio and began chatting with the audience about how "*The Tom Green Show* does not do poo-poo humor" while waving the excrement around in the faces of the audience. One fan, thinking it was a fake prop, touched the pile Tom was holding and found out first-hand that the excrement was quite real! Tom then walked over to the set and tucked the refuse into a frilly pink Barbie bed set up on his desk, and then started the show. Apparently The Comedy Network agreed with Ed's stand on poo-poo humor because they too did not want to encourage toilet chuckles. "When he has it in his hands and is walking around with it, it got to be so extreme that it was a gross-out factor that was crossing the line," said Ed. Flushing that episode down the toilet, *The Tom Green Show* completed production of the 13 episodes in two jam-packed weekends. With editing wrapped up and the crew taking a small break, Tom waited for his initiation into the world of national talk-show fame.

As an omen of the crazy and incredible days to come, *The Tom Green Show* premiered on The Comedy Network on Friday, February 13, 1998. The host, noticeably haggard from weeks in the editing suites and thin from stress, was in heaven watching his little cable show take hold of a national audience. Fans from across the country identified with his style and fell in love with his off-the-wall sense of humor. "I'm still not sure what it is about what Tom does that the audience is seeking," confessed Ed. "I'm not confessing that I understand it. I just know that there is some connection to the younger age group, teens to early twenties, the late high school to university crowd. I think it's all part of that 'throwing rocks at tradition,' going against the norm, that is part of the connection."

Whatever the connection, Tom loved every minute of the attention. Each time he crossed the line his fans were hysterical with laughter. The segments where Tom mocked authority figures had the biggest impact on his audience. He was fulfilling their dreams by challenging authority and getting away with it. They applauded each and every time he was thrown out of a store, shopping mall, or museum. "Scuba Hood" and "Buying Condoms" are two of those unforgettable skits. Dressed in full scuba gear — flippers, face mask, and air tank — Tom splashed his way in and out of wishing fountains in an Ottawa mall. Tom was Scuba

DUNDAS ST. E. 1

WINTER BLOWOUT WINTER BLOWOUT WINTER BLOWOUT WINTER BLOWOUT WINTER BLOWOUT WINTER BLOWOUT WINTER BLOWOUT

GREEN BAY ACKERS

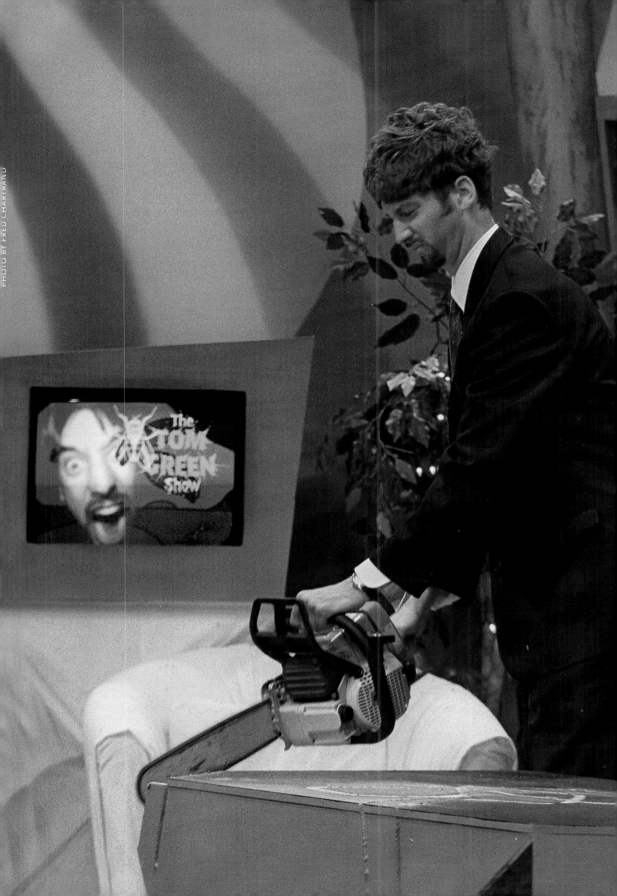

The TOM GREEN Show

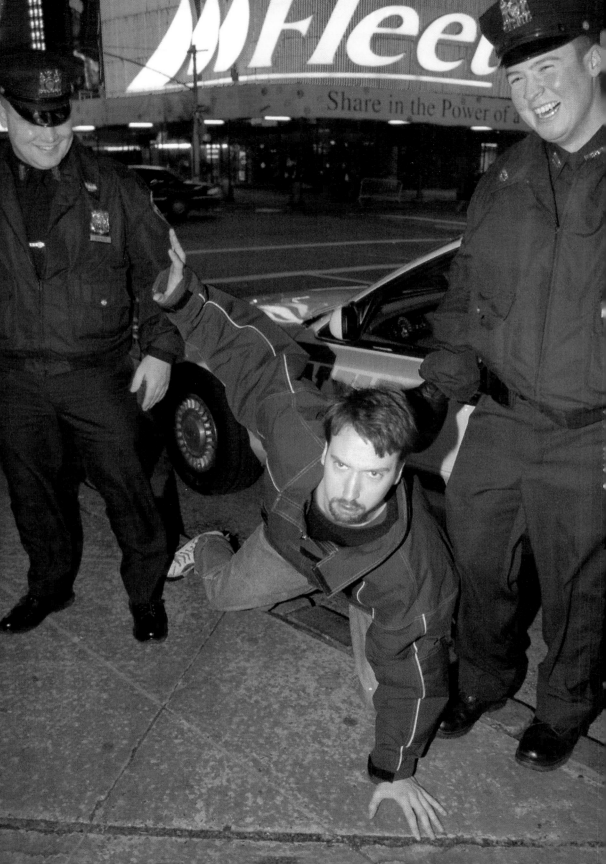

Hood and, in a reversal of the classic tale, he would steal from the poor by fishing the coins from the fountain and give the money back to the rich by depositing it in the bank. Tom had a ball shocking mall shoppers who were calmly lunching in the food court; he had them in stitches trying to figure out just exactly what he was doing. "We wanted to get people's reaction, surprise and catch them off guard," he said describing his technique. It wasn't only the shoppers who took notice of his hijinks. The security guards patrolling the mall were stunned to see Scuba Hood swimming in their fountains. Not knowing what to make of the aquatic intruder, the guards used their authority to throw him out of the mall and actually ban him from future visits. "The security guards came up and got mad 'cause we were in the fountain in the mall and they were grabbing me and kicking me out, and people eating in the food court were going, 'What the hell, there's a guy in scuba gear jumping in the fountain,'" Tom laughed. It was the bizarre reaction of the shoppers in the mall that fueled his comedy. The more they laughed and the more involved they got in his plans, the crazier the joke became.

That's what happened during his stunt to purchase condoms, too. We expect people buying condoms to be timid and embarrassed that the clerk knows what they're buying them for. Tom, on the other hand, burst into the drugstore and walked up to the pharmacy counter carrying a chainsaw motor and started explaining why he needed to buy condoms. "I've got to go buy some condoms because I'm going to be doing some work underwater," he explained straight-faced to the cashier. "I need to waterproof my hands and I don't want to use latex gloves to waterproof my hands 'cause I'm working with a piece of machinery and I don't want to get my fingers caught inside the grooves."

The noise of the growling chainsaw and the heavy gasoline fumes distracted and bewildered the employees. "I don't want them for sex," he said, chiding the clerk. "I just want to waterproof my arms." Walking through the store, he explained the whole scenario to any shoppers who would listen. He even talked one counter clerk into helping him get the condom on his hand. Tormenting dozens of shoppers and store workers, Tom was finally told by one shopkeeper to take his motor out of the store and hit the road. He was getting used to being thrown out of stores and shopping malls. It was becoming a big part of his game.

The Comedy Network hoped the spontaneous nature of *The Tom Green Show* would appeal to their new national audience. When Ed Robinson purchased the show he took a gamble, hoping it would mix well with the foreign properties he put into the schedule. It was exactly what he was looking for in terms of raw Canadian talent. Tom's humor was off-the-cuff, funny, and irreverent, and it challenged what conventional broadcasters were putting on the air. Ed loved the format of the show and believed in its cast. They were all hard-working, dynamic young comedians who had earned this shot at fame. All he had to do was help deliver their humor across the country.

6

TURNING GREEN

When his producer, Merilyn Read, informed Tom the show was going national, he decided his personality should follow suit. His big opportunity came when a movie crew arrived in town with some very famous people in tow. Tom saw it as an opportunity to get his mug exposed to the right sort of Hollywood types — or at least that was what he had planned. What really happened was that his photo ended up gracing the pages of a late May 1998 edition of the tabloid magazine *National Enquirer,* a commemorative issue honoring the legendary Frank Sinatra. The *Enquirer* had gotten hold of a cheeky photo of Tom snuggling up to James Bond heartthrob Pierce Brosnan.

Brosnan, recognized for his roles in *Dante's Peak*, *The Mirror Has Two Faces*, *The Thomas Crown Affair*, and a string of Bond flicks, traveled to Chelsea, Quebec, in the spring of 1998 for the filming of *Grey Owl*, a $30-million film directed by the Oscar-winning Richard Attenborough. *Grey Owl*, as described by *Ottawa Citizen* film critic Jay Stone, is the true life story of British-born Archie Belaney. "Belaney came to Canada in the 1920s and reinvented himself as Grey Owl, a half-breed trapper and guide," wrote Stone. "Belaney passed himself off as a native and became an expert in wilderness lore and a leading environmentalist. It was not until his death in 1938 that his double life became known."

The picturesque town of Chelsea was transformed into a 1930s fur-trading village for the shoot. During the months prior to filming, swarthy leading man Brosnan learned how to canoe, snowshoe, throw a knife, and shoot a gun. He even went so far as to grow out his normally short, dark coif. The hair flowing down past his shoulders was neatly tied in long braids that complemented the traditional buckskin costume he wore as Grey Owl.

During the short time they were filming in Chelsea, both Attenborough and Brosnan were hounded by the local media trying to get an interview, a photo, or even a glimpse of the stars. To the chagrin of his fans, Brosnan remained well guarded during his stay. It wasn't until the final day of filming that set coordinators organized a press conference for Brosnan. "The welcome of the people in this community has been great. It's knocked my socks off," Pierce told a hoard of reporters, including Jackie Leroux of the *Ottawa Sun*. "Everyone's been very respectful of us. They've embraced us and welcomed us. I've had a very comfortable time here. I've had nothing to complain about. This week has just been one of those magical weeks." He politely fielded a stream of questions from local media types about everything from the long locks he grew out for the movie to how he felt about starring in another Bond flick. But he was caught completely off guard when a mysterious-looking figure stepped out of the crowd and rushed to his side carrying a guitar. Before he could figure out what was happening, Brosnan was face-to-face with Ottawa loony Tom Green. Green, taking a moment to acknowledge the crowd of reporters, grabbed hold of his guitar and dropped into a rocking chair to perform a little ditty entitled "Pierce Is a Gorgeous Man."

After the song was completed to his satisfaction, Tom put down the guitar and officially welcomed Brosnan to the Ottawa region: "Pierce, thank you for coming to our city." Brosnan didn't have time to react before Tom moved closer and planted a juicy kiss on the puzzled actor's face. The flash from the many cameras catching this bizarre moment was blinding. Once laughter from the crowd had subsided, Brosnan turned to the budding songbird and replied with a laugh, "You poor boy, Tom. Don't give up your day job" (Leroux). What Brosnan didn't know was that this *was* Tom's day job.

✷

After a sweet serenade, Tom cozies up to Pierce Brosnan
JONATHAN HAYWARD / *OTTAWA SUN*

The saying "anything goes" never had more significance than when *The Tom Green Show* made its Canada-wide debut on The Comedy Network. Its time slot, safely after family viewing hours, allowed more freedom to expand the boundaries of its comedy than the gang could have ever anticipated. Suddenly even the most outrageous and grotesque stunts were considered potential material for the show. In fact, the more obscene the better. Tom and Derek, as the main writers for the show, explored the devious and deranged recesses of their minds. The results defied the laws of socially acceptable behavior and often focused on their unrelenting fascination with roadkill. These dead critters, cast away on the sides of highways and back roads, were revered mascots of *The Tom Green Show,* celebrated more in death than they could ever have expected in life.

The show's original mascot, Skinny, had met an untimely death after being accidentally thrown from his roaming grounds on Tom's turfed desk, so the gang went in search of another beastly mascot to represent the show. It appeared in the form of one of "the most beautiful and gorgeous" pieces of roadkill, according to set coordinator Danielle Lacelle. "It was so striking that people didn't believe it was real," she remarked. The raccoon, affectionately nicknamed Racky, was kept on the set during taping and stored on Tom's apartment balcony in the off-season. Racky was the running joke for the better part of a season and he turned up in some very precarious places, including as an uninvited guest on the talk show *Open Mike with Mike Bullard* in November of 1998.

The Masonic Temple in downtown Toronto, where *Open Mike* is taped, has been a landmark in the city for decades. A familiar venue for concert-goers, the Temple is loved by artists and audience members alike for the great acoustics around the main stage. Housing the Comedy Channel's *Open Mike*, the Temple attracts a new type of audience. The floor space, once a mosh pit for rock fans, is organized to accommodate comedy fans attending the performance. The auditorium is filled with rows of chairs both on the floor and in the balcony framing the upper section across from the stage. This is where Mike Bullard goes to work, performing his opening monologue to applause and hollering from the jam-packed audience.

On this chilly November evening he was interviewing actress Melissa DiMarco from the Canadian drama series *Riverdale* before introducing prankster Tom Green. "Whenever Tom shows up for an interview, 70% of the audience is mine and 30% of it is his," Mike said, confessing that the security team is always worried about the Tom Green fans and what they are capable of doing. When introduced, Tom sauntered out onto the stage carrying a suitcase. Plunking himself down in the chair beside DiMarco, he set the bag down in front of Bullard on the host's desk. "I knew what was in the bag as soon as he set it down on the desk," proclaimed Bullard. "Just the way it lay, you could almost hear a mush when he set it down." Suspecting something of the "dead animal" sort but not knowing quite what Tom had in mind, Bullard played along with the stunt. After spending years in the business and working the comedy circuit at Yuk Yuk's clubs nationwide, there wasn't much that could catch him off guard. But if anyone was capable of surprising him, Tom Green was the man for the job. "What I've found out is that you don't interview Tom on the air, you just roll with the punches," admitted Bullard.

There was no way he could have prepared for the extremely grotesque stunt Tom had in mind that night. While being interviewed on the live-to-tape program Green innocently reached into the sack he'd brought with him and pulled out the rotting carcasses of a raccoon and squirrel. As soon as Bullard saw the writhing maggots crawling out of the dead animals' nostrils and mouths he literally lost it. "I ran out into the back alley to throw up," he admitted with a laugh. "I threw up for 10 minutes and they had to stop taping for the first time ever on our show."

While Bullard was flying out the backstage door, DiMarco bolted from her seat to get away from the repulsive scene. The audience, wriggling themselves, were completely surprised by what was happening. There was a frenzy of activity onstage as a slew of directors, producers, and stage hands scrambled to restore order to the chaotic situation. Seated in the audience, Merilyn and Danielle couldn't help but grin at the panicked reaction of the crew. "It was so crazy," Danielle said, reminiscing. "There was a craze as staff members bounced into action armed with air fresheners. The whole staff was going nuts." Twenty minutes passed

Mike Bullard is revolted by Tom's love of roadkill (November, 1988)
JAMES HOLLOWAY / *TORONTO SUN*

before Bullard, still choking, regained his composure and returned to the stage to restore control of the crowd. "It was the most rancid thing I've ever smelled in my life," he explained. "It was like a corpse." In fact as the hot studio lights continued to blare down on the roadkill still lying limply in the center of Bullard's desk, the stench was growing even more overpowering.

Once the animals were safely out of the host's sight, taping resumed, and so too did the anarchy. Tom wasn't finished playing with Bullard just yet. As Mike tried to carry on with the show, introducing the night's final guests, the Rheostatics, Green repeatedly threw himself at the slightly annoyed host. "At that point, I could have bench-pressed 400 pounds," Mike noted to the *Toronto Sun*'s Claire Bickley, saying he grabbed the out-of-control Green and stuck him into a headlock. He wrestled Tom to the ground under his desk — much to the disapproval of die-hard Green fans, who shouted their displeasure by screaming obscenities in Bullard's direction. Security guards swiftly removed them from the theater.

When the mayhem finally subsided and taping wrapped, Mike was more than a little relieved that the interview was over. It had been a rough night, but surprisingly enough he wasn't the least bit irritated at the way it all unfolded. "I don't get mad at him; that's probably the reason he likes me so much," boasted Bullard from the *Open Mike* offices in the Temple. In fact, Mike explained that the only words of anger came from Tom himself, who was disappointed Bullard stepped off-screen to blow chunks. "He wanted me to vomit on camera," laughed Bullard. He offered Green a friendly tip in exchange for the dead animal carcass: "If you're going to do something like that, have a joke to go with it, not just a dead raccoon." The following day, after the *Open Mike* maggot fiasco, the Masonic Temple was vacated and a professional fumigating team was hired to clean and disinfect the theater space at a cost of close to $4,000.

All joking aside, this wasn't the first time Green had been the cause of mayhem and a hefty price tag while making an appearance on Bullard's show. During one of Mike's first interviews, around Christmas 1997, the budding prankster cost the *Open Mike* production team $6,000 for a new microphone when a milk prank went berserk. In one of his trademark stunts, Green brought along a bag of milk and performed what he affectionately calls the "Jugs of Juice" gag. He punched holes into the bags and squirted the white juice around the room. Not only did Tom spray the furniture, the cameras and the host, but he also managed to cream one of the costly microphones. "See, my big problem is keeping the crew from killing him after the show," remarked Bullard, who feels the need to protect Green when security is close. "The only reason they don't is because they know I like him, but whenever he's here security and the crew want to kill him."

But it was Bullard who ended up with the upper hand, getting some revenge the third time Tom appeared on his program. After being introduced, Tom walked demurely out onto the stage toting two large suitcases, one of which was handcuffed to his wrist. He called to Mike, "I brought you a present, I brought you a nice present." To which Mike, taking into consideration Tom's previous appearances on the show, asked, "It's not one thing cut in half, is it?" Tom was quick to offer reassurances that the prank would not send Bullard running out to the back alley for a repeat performance. "Because last time I came on I brought a gross present and I feel really bad about it," Tom said, sincerity dripping from his words. Mike replied, "Tom, you know, after seven or eight days and a few shots I forgot all about it."

Satisfied with Mike's reaction, Tom set his sights on the luggage. Fumbling momentarily to unlock the handcuffs, he set his wrist free and tried to spring the locks on the bags, but they wouldn't give. "It's not a mean present," Tom said with a haggard look on his face. Still trying to break open the lock, he hoisted the bag over his head and threw it crashing to the ground, but the lock still wouldn't budge. Unfazed by the incident, Tom pulled a gas-powered chainsaw out of the second bag. Pumping and yanking at the chainsaw's pull cord, Tom was encouraged by the chanting of the crowd. Mike quickly realized that there was no way he was going to get the chainsaw to start humming. "He ran out of gas," explained Bullard. "It leaked out of the tank and all over the suitcase." Mike could tell by the way Tom was acting that he was both frustrated and disappointed the stunt wasn't going according to plan, so Mike dove in to help out. He threw the baggage against the desk repeatedly before being rescued by a crew member who handed the duo a small

Tom greets his adoring fans at the filming of Open Mike
PHOTO BY DANIELLE LACELLE

knife. After slicing cleanly through the canvas coating, Tom reached in
and pulled out a bouquet of flowers and a box of chocolates from the
mangled suitcase. "Oh, Tommy," Mike said with a smile crossing his
face. Tom responded, "I love you, Mike," which the talk show host took
to heart as he planted a smooch on the comedian's lips. Now back in
his element, Tom pulled Mike close in a warm embrace and sensually
kissed his face, slowly moving his tongue to nuzzle Mike's earlobe. In a
mock fit of passion the two threw themselves down on the desk with
Mike lying on top of Tom, who was still gyrating from all the excitement.
This playful sexual exchange may have made Tom infamous as the most
outrageous guest ever to appear on the *Open Mike* show, but it wasn't
the first time his work lead him into some very heated exchanges.

∗

The blaring sirens echoed along Cyrville Road as a stream of fire trucks
maneuvered their way through the steady flow of rush-hour traffic. Looking up to the sky, firefighters followed the clouds of billowing black

smoke as they rolled across that stretch of the Queensway. The fire was already fully ensconced and in danger of spreading quickly through an entire storage facility, once used as a lumberyard. The aerial ladder and three pumper trucks pulled up in the parking lot. Seeing the roaring flames and thick, black smoke, the firemen instantly sprang into action. "We were only on the scene for a few moments when the front wall of the building blew out. There were bricks flying everywhere," recalled fireman Dean Foster. Within seconds the entire front face of the building, a storage space for paper products, was destroyed, and the firemen rushed along to the side of the building to open a wall in order to try and contain the blaze. Armed with axes and saws, Foster's team worked diligently to cut through the layers of construction material. They stopped when they heard voices from the side of the building, only a few feet away from the inferno. "I thought it looked like Tom Green, and I asked the guy I was working with if he thought it was him 'cause he was literally standing under a wall of fire," said Foster. "It was a pretty dangerous spot and as soon as I saw the video camera I knew it was Tom Green."

With the blaze growing in intensity at an alarming rate, the firemen, wearing standard heavy bunker gear, were soon drenched with perspiration, their faces marked with black soot from the blaze. This was one of the most serious fires of the year and it was a major job just to get it under control. It took more than five hours to subdue. Although the situation was serious, some of the firefighters couldn't help but smile at what happened as they continued to fight the flames. "I found it humorous when fellow fireman Grant Anderson headed back to the truck to refill his air pack and Tom stopped him and asked, 'Did you file your income tax return?'" said Foster. The question was so out of place, catching Anderson by surprise, that Foster says he replied in a astonished tone "Yes!" to which Tom redirected, "Are you expecting a refund?" Still not knowing what to make of the jokester carrying the microphone, Anderson retaliated, "I hope so!" before rushing back to help his fellow firefighters.

The presence of Green at the fiery scene was more than comical, and it caught most of them off guard. They didn't know what to make of him. "I was so involved with the events of the fire that seeing him set me back for 15 to 20 seconds," confessed platoon chief Mickey Stackpole, the senior officer in charge that day. "As soon as I realized what he was doing I got a real chuckle out of it. He was kind of saying to us, 'C'mon, lighten up, boys!'" After chatting with Anderson and a few other firemen about their income tax returns, Green set his sights a small distance away from the flames, walking up to one of the captains and posing the same questions.

"At that point he was disrupting the work the firemen were doing and it was becoming both hazardous to his health and theirs," said one by-stander who had watched from a safe distance. "The police were there investigating some kids who they thought were responsible for the accident, and they were asked to escort Mr. Green out of the immediate area." Tom was guided off the premises on the arms of two police officers. He happily left the scene, knowing full well he'd gotten the segment footage he needed. He was used to being asked to leave, and knew that eventually someone would draw the line when he was no longer just funny, but becoming a nuisance.

There was another time when Tom joined firefighters as they tried to tame an out-of-control blaze. On a filming expedition, *The Tom Green Show* ventured out onto city streets in search of interesting objects to catch on tape. Driving along in their car, which was loaded with a slew of possible props to use for stunts, they came across a fire truck stopped at the side of a home with firefighters busy unloading their equipment. Seeing an opportunity for humor, Tom grabbed a fire extinguisher from the trunk of the car and walked up to the firefighters. He repeatedly offered his assistance, and the fire extinguisher, to the firemen — to no avail. Getting no response, Green redirected his attention to the crowd of gawkers watching from across the street. Shouting to the crowd with the aid of a megaphone he'd also grabbed from the prop car, he said, "We've got the whole situation under control."

These brushes with flames are just a few examples of the great lengths Tom will go to get a laugh. He has no fear when it comes to his comedy and often puts himself in harm's way just to get a chuckle out of his fans. For him fire is a perfect medium — it offers an element of both surprise and danger — and is often used in his skits. None of his fans were shocked when they saw him running down the streets of Ottawa with flames nipping at his ankles, directing motorists to their destinations in the episode "Burning Feet Man." Once the shot was filmed he fell to the sidewalk screaming for a shot from the fire extinguisher. He'll do anything for a laugh.

*

While Tom was looking to challenge the borders of conventional comedy with his humor, the stunts being performed on the show were becoming more and more risqué and very shocking to audiences. Although Tom adamantly denounces the label "shock comic," he is very comfortable with the obscene and vulgar situations he creates. The show's late time slot coupled with the mandate of The Comedy Network, gave Derek and Tom more freedom to explore new areas of their minds for materials, wading through an abyss of colorful characters and discarded roadkill — including a dead moose they found on a road trip to Calgary. Driving past the large animal, which lay sprawled out on the ground at the side of the highway, Tom pulled their van to a stop and got an idea for a segment — to try and revive the expired creature. Walking up to it, Tom called out to the rotting carcass, "C'mon, wake up, wake up!" When his pleading didn't work, Tom opted for a different approach. Straddling the moose, he explained the "situation" to nearby construction workers: "I was just driving along and I was trying to open up a can of juice and adjust my radio at the same time and then all of a sudden this thing jumps out of the woods." Tom emphatically described the measures they could use to help save the animal as the construction workers stared at him in amazement. Setting his pelvis in motion he began gyrating on top of the dead animal. "I'm going to hump it like this," he called out to the shocked road crew, motioning to the lower portion of his anatomy. "You've got to give it mouth-to-mouth . . . we can help him!" he cried out as the workers walked away in disgust.

A few months later the "moose humping" episode surfaced on *The Tom Green Show* for the benefit of guest Don Cuddy, an ecologist with the Ministry of Natural Resources in Canada. Tom rolled the clip of his tireless efforts to resuscitate the moose as Cuddy watched from his seat. He was surprised, to say the least, at what was going on and had to fake a smile. Cuddy, whose expertise lies in the examination of rare and endangered species, thought he was asked onto the show to discuss extinction. "They told me it was a comedy show, but that there would be a serious segment and I was there to talk about extinct animals," explained Cuddy. "I'm not hung up too much on dead animals, but when he showed me the clip I thought it was really strange.

"He brought out this dead raccoon and I thought, 'OK, he's launching into the topic of endangered species by first talking about animals that *are not* on the list,'" said Cuddy, recalling the interview with a somewhat sour taste in his mouth. "When he brought out the raccoon I waited for the serious discussion to start, but we never got there." What happened instead was enough to make even the moose turn over in its grave. Tom questioned Don about the legalities of taking home a dead animal from the roadway. Feeling guilty, Tom said he wanted to make amends for trying to hump the dead animal and brought out a Tupperware container that was hiding under his desk. Opening the dish, he explained that its contents — a dead raccoon — were found on the road and he wanted to return the body to the Ministry of Natural Resources. To ensure the carcass would keep until Cuddy appeared on the show, Tom had stored the critter in his freezer. "Being that it was kept in the freezer I just figured I would thaw it out for you before we give it back, so it's in the natural state we found it in," Tom said before shoving the animal into a prop microwave oven behind his desk.

Cuddy, seated beside Tom on the stage, watched as he poked and prodded the raccoon, trying to stuff it inside the tiny oven. "I never in my wildest dreams would have thought that's what we would be talking about on the show," admitted Cuddy, who had prepared for the interview by extensively studying animals on the endangered species list from Canada and the United States. "I thought it was going to be a serious discussion, but that couldn't have been farther from the truth."

Placing ordinary people into bizarre situations is what stimulates Tom and Derek and gets their creative juices flowing. A good example of their efforts was the segment "Glenn's Bum." The two coerced Glenn's quiet and complacent onstage character to drop his drawers for Tom, exposing his naked behind — and a makeshift tattoo of Tom saying "Tom 4 Ever" — for the studio audience. Then, mocking the portly cohost, Tom pulled out his guitar and serenaded Glenn's buttocks with an original ditty,

"Children, They Make Me Smile." Snuggling up close to his subject, Tom had his half-naked muse petrified he was going to put his fingers on the exposed skin. "Wait a minute, we had a deal. *No touching*," Glenn wailed to the guitar-strumming Green. "I'm walking around with my ass exposed and you're touching it!" Once Glenn was convinced Tom didn't want to place his fingers anywhere near his bottom, the sing-along resumed. "Children, they make me smile, they make the world go 'round," Tom crooned as Glenn's bum wriggled around to the music. As Tom edged his way closer to his backside, Glenn continually shot warnings in Tom's direction reminding him of the no-touch policy. "Do you think I want to touch that?" Tom retaliated with a laugh. "I can't believe you think I'm going to put my face in your ass!" What did Glenn have to worry about? After all, the two had carried human excrement from the washroom together and made each other vomit to the delight of their fans.

*

From microwaving roadkill to bashing the brains out of a dead cow to create his own "cow brain boat," Tom goes to great lengths to conjure up amusing activities for his fans, giving them something new and creative to watch on the tube. Tuning in to the show each week there is one thing for certain — you never know what to expect.

This was the exact feeling his parents had when Tom arrived at their home at 3 a.m. This wake-up call apparently came from the Godfather; Tom deposited a bloody cow's head on their bedspread, spouting the phrase, "This is a message from Don Corleone." He recited the words to his parents' sleeping figures. "It says Luca Brasi sleeps with the fishes!" Sleepy-eyed and unaware of what was happening in their bedroom, the Greens' first reaction was anger as they saw the bright red splotches of blood on their comforter. The severed cow's skull lay lifeless on the sheets. "It was really gross," Tom's mom, Mary Jane Green, said, recalling watching Sport, the family dog, lapping up the dripping blood. "It was like *The Godfather* and the horse head, only he couldn't get a horse's head so of course he got a cow's head."

Fully awake as the camera lights zoomed in on their shocked faces,

Richard and Mary Jane soon kicked Tom and his entourage out of their bedroom. Once again the Greens tried to get back to sleep, only to be bombarded in their dreams with visions of their eldest son and the pranks he'd pulled on them in the past. They never knew when he was going to strike, wreaking havoc in their lives. But the one thing they were certain of was that he always had some new prank in the works, and it was only a matter of time before he struck again.

7

MAD FOR PLAID

It's 3 a.m. Do you know where your children are? For Richard and Mary Jane Green that was always a loaded question. When they did know the whereabouts of their son Tom, it usually meant he was about to burst into their bedroom in the wee hours of the morning to snuggle up between them. And we all know it was not for a kiss goodnight.

Tom has become the poster child for parentally harassed kids everywhere. He is a hero to young fans who dream of getting even with their parents for endless chores, strict curfews, and chiding remarks like "Why don't you just get a job?" and "Have you finished your homework?" Tom is idolized for his ingenious ability to seek revenge on his parents in the most ironic ways, making it his job to annoy and disrupt their lives. In fact, he has made a career of revenge and it certainly has been sweet.

Whenever ideas for skits were running dry, he'd pop into his parents' home and disrupt their world. The premise for the skits usually came from Tom's memories of growing up; he would take things his parents said to him as a young boy and turn them around. He has made a mockery of his parents by giving them starring roles in his quest for stardom. They have became his muses, and the butt of some of his most famous jokes. While most fans of the show think his very public pranks on his own family are hilarious, Tom's detractors criticize him for biting the hands that fed him. What they don't realize is that Tom has discovered a secret about his parents. Although they are usually initially angry at the pranks, their outrage eventually subsides, and, Tom speculates, "they actually get off on it most of the time."

Right from the beginning Richard and Mary Jane were given a baptism by fire where their son's career was concerned. At the age of 23, his first year on Rogers Community TV, Tom proved to his parents that he would go to great lengths to impress his fans. The very first stunt he pulled was when his parents went on a 10-day canoe trip through picturesque Algonquin Park with some close friends. Ideally the vacation was a way for the group to get away from the stresses of city life, to relax and get back to nature. Like most parents, Richard and Mary Jane laid down the law before they left on the trip. No parties. No mischief. And, most importantly, they handed him a long list of chores which were to be completed before their return. In a touching moment caught on tape, Tom put a loving arm around his father's shoulder and in all sincerity told him he was going to go above and beyond the call of duty and make them proud. They happily — but not so wisely — placed their trust and confidence in Tom as they headed out of town. What they didn't know was that Tom had other plans in store for his parents that had nothing to do with household chores.

After 10 days of trekking through the wilderness of Algonquin Park, all Richard and Mary Jane could think about on their return was hopping into hot showers to get rid of the week's worth of dirt from roughing it in the bush. They were relaxed and content as they drove down the familiar streets of their neighborhood. But as soon as they pulled into their own driveway, a throbbing headache surfaced on Mary Jane's forehead and the scowl returned to Richard's face. "What's going on?" Richard demanded as he shut off the car. "I just don't believe this," Mary Jane chimed in as she climbed out from the passenger side of the car. They were completely stunned as they stared at their once-pristine white-paneled home with delicate rose-colored shutters flanking the windows. The address on the front door was correct, but the house that stood before them was most certainly not theirs. This house was an eyesore, painted multiple shades of purple, green, blue, and brown in an attention-grabbing tartan design.

"Oh my God," were all the words they could muster. They were not amused. This was not what they had in mind when they asked Tom to take care of the house. Before they had time to regain their composure from the initial shock, Tom appeared on the front lawn with a video camera to capture their reactions. Mary Jane was the first to break down, bursting into tears. "I just sort of locked myself in the bathroom, which I tended to do very often because I didn't want a camera in my face," she confided during an interview in the fall of 1998.

Infuriated by the plaid house and tired from a long road trip, the Greens were in no mood for Tom's jokes. When Mary Jane resurfaced from her hiding place in the bathroom later that evening, she was relieved to find the house painted back to its original colors. But Tom was in serious trouble this time and his parents were definitely going to punish him. They were not in the mood to put up with stunts like this. The following week they grounded him from using his car and took away the keys. "That'll show him who's boss," they thought. "He'll think twice before pulling something like this again."

But it didn't take Tom long to realize that the gags that got the biggest reaction from his fans and the ones the majority of his audience could relate to were those where he used his parents as the punch line for his jokes. The terrorizing of the Greens was just beginning.

✳

As most of his fans are aware, Tom is a lover of all animals — dead or alive. For the most part he believes it's a hereditary trait because both his parents adore their furry household pets. They feel having pets in their lives helps them cope with stress. Which started Tom thinking — if his parents love animals so much and they help relieve the stress in their lives, then they should have more animals. Period. One Friday afternoon, with seemingly good-hearted intentions, Tom ventured to a petting farm to look for some new baby animals to add to the Green family. He scouted out the barnyard looking for the perfect animals to match his parents' personalities. He wandered through the fields asking the animals, "Do you like parents? Do you like parents?" Those that answered the question — two dozen animals including a donkey, goats, ducks, chickens, and a llama — were adopted as new members of his clan.

Anticipating his parents' excitement Tom rushed back home to prepare the house for the arrival of the menagerie. Looking to be the responsible son, Tom went to great lengths to create a barnyard atmosphere for the new pets. He safely stored his mother's living room knick-knacks and family photos out of the way of pounding hooves and curious nibbling. He put down a thick layer of plastic sheeting to coat the floor, walls, and living room couch from any untimely and smelly accidents. He finished off the room with a plush blanket over the protective layer to make the animals as comfortable as possible. The animals were paraded into the home two by two, like a recreation of Noah's ark. They then began curiously exploring their new dwelling. Meanwhile, a small crowd of the Greens' longtime neighbors gathered on their front lawns to watch the procession and await the arrival of Richard and Mary Jane. In the house Tom greeted his furry friends with a fitting welcome. Acting as an example for the pets, he crawled around on the floor animal-style crying out, "I like to lie down cozy on the floor and Mommy and Daddy will come home and they'll see their new babies."

With the animals grazing on the floor of the Greens' bungalow and the cameras ready to roll, all that was missing were Tom's parents. And wouldn't they be surprised! His father was the first to arrive shortly after 3 p.m. as he did every afternoon. Walking up the front steps he could have sworn he heard the "baaa, baaa" of a sheep coming from his living room. "No, that's impossible," he said to himself, turning the doorknob. The door opened a crack and jammed up against something inside. Pushing harder, the door gave way and flew open, leaving him standing face-to-face with . . . a llama. "For Chrissake, what are you doing?" Richard said to Tom as the video camera followed him into the house. Shaking his head in disbelief, Richard slowly turned the corner of the hallway to peer inside the living room. He was stopped in his tracks by the sight of all the animals roaming around the room.

"It was quite a zoo," said Richard, recalling the incident with a smile. "We were just lucky he remembered to put the plastic down because they were in there for quite a while and it could have been a real mess." Although his father's reaction was quite vocal regarding the living room zoo, Tom would not be satisfied until his mother was also caught on tape. After all, she was always more outspoken regarding his videotaping stunts and the disruption he caused in their lives.

While Tom was busy getting his dad acquainted with the new babies, Mary Jane called from the office to let them know they would have to fend for themselves for dinner because she was working late and wouldn't be home until after 8 p.m. Tom began to panic. What if his mom didn't get home in time to see what he'd done to their living room? He had to make sure she would be home in the next few hours or the joke would be ruined. There was only one way to get his mom home: he'd have to get his dad to call her at the office. Although he was furious, Richard still had to laugh at the scene — animals sauntering around the house while Tom fed them animal crackers. It was enough to make anyone laugh and he felt certain Mary Jane would too. Not wanting to spend the evening alone watching the animals urinate on their living room floor, Richard placed a desperate phone call to his wife, pleading with her to come home early. He told her it was *important*, but Mary Jane was adamant that she was staying at work. "I think it would be a good idea if you come home," he said to her. "You should really come home!" It wasn't until the third phone call that Richard had successfully piqued the interest of his wife and she headed home. Not knowing what to expect, but certain she was in for some prank, Mary Jane walked tentatively into her home at around 6 p.m. She was fully prepared to be entertained.

"Never in a hundred years would I have expected that there would be a zoo in my living room," she said, looking back at the chaotic situation. "But actually they were kind of cute." At that point the animals had been cooped up in the small living room for more than three hours. The smell of urine was overwhelming as she sat on the couch and hand-fed the creatures animal crackers while she scolded Tom for dropping some of the cookies on the floor. "You're mad 'cause I'm spilling animal crackers? There's crap all over the floor," Tom said with a chuckle.

In spite of the stench and crumbs throughout the house, Mary Jane found it hard not to laugh and thought it was a little ironic that Tom had thought to put dropcloths down to protect the floors. "It was so unlike his normal behavior," she confided about her son's poor history of tidying up after himself. "When he lived at home he had a real flaw about cleaning up his room and stuff. He had things all over the house." This messy animal joke got Mary Jane to thinking. If more stunts like this one were going to take place, she thought, she should consider tiling the entire first floor and installing a drain in the middle of the living room. "It would be so much easier just to hose everything down," she said. "But I'm afraid that would just encourage him."

Once filming for the "zoo" segment was complete, the Greens stepped outside on the front lawn for a much-needed breath of fresh air. To their surprise they weren't the only ones present. There was a scattering of neighbors sitting in their lawn chairs, eager to find out just what exactly was going on inside the Green home. "At first I thought it was kind of funny," recalls Richard. "When I had arrived home and they were sitting in their lawn chairs I thought they wanted to come over for a swim." But it wasn't the enticement of a refreshing dip in the Greens' backyard pool that caught the attention of Helmut and Gisele Wewer and their relatives visiting from Germany.

"Our visitors didn't want to leave until Richard and Mary Jane came home; they wanted to see their reaction," said Gisele. "We watched the whole afternoon as they prepared the house and we just couldn't believe that he did the whole thing without them knowing. It was hilarious." For the following week the Greens' neighbors kept a watchful eye on the home, just to see what Tom would do to his parents next. But to their disappointment, all the neighbors saw were the windows of the Green house flung wide open in an attempt to rid the first floor of the smell of animal urine and droppings. Tom's intentions in offering more animals to his parents had backfired — instead of alleviating some of the stress in their lives, he had doubled it.

✱

Dez Fitzgerald is an artist. His love of painting, however, is expressed on automobiles rather than the more traditional canvas. It was during the early 1970s that Dez had to make the choice whether or not to follow his artistic passion. It was either head to college or follow through with painting. The choice was obvious to him. "In the '70s the van business really boomed. There was a lot of painting of murals and all the air brushing, so I got sidetracked." Aside from a few semi-nude pictures for a couple of motorcycle guys, Dez's auto artwork remained on the tame side for most of his career. *Most* of his career, that is, because after he met Tom Green he could no longer say he'd never drawn explicit pictures. It was a meeting he will never forget.

One afternoon Tom made his way to the industrial sector of the small rural town of Greely, just outside Ottawa, looking specifically for Dez's Paint Shop. He bounded from his car with a goofy grin on his face and walked into the double garage of Dez's auto center. "He asked if I would paint a nude picture on the hood of his father's car for his television show, so I said OK," Dez said, fondly remembering the meeting. Tom filled Dez in on the joke. He wanted a permanent air-brush drawing of two fully involved lesbians painted on a replica hood of the family car. The idea was he would swap the fake hood for the real one and video-tape their reactions. The skit would be known as the "Slut Mobile." "My first impression of him? I thought he was strange and eccentric. I had said I could make the photo a bit blurry and hide some of the nasty parts," said Dez, pointing to a picture of the car hood on a filing cabi-net in his office. "But he said no. He wanted it just like the picture."

Without blushing or feeling even the slightest bit uncomfortable at the sexual nature of the photo, Dez went to work on the 12-hour-long project. The picture for the $400 gag was first outlined on the replica hood and the remaining artwork was a freehand drawing using the air-brush technique.

As news of the controversial hood spread throughout the industrial park, Dez's Paint Shop soon became a hangout for local business-people. Every day a small crowd gathered to watch his progress. "I had an audience of five or six people on different days standing around tell-ing me how I should go about things to make it anatomically correct," laughed Dez. "I wasn't concerned about the nature of the picture, I only told him I wouldn't put my name on it." Although Dez chose not to take credit for the explicit hood, he couldn't help but check out the final product Tom came up with to fool his parents. "It was great," he said, admitting to be a casual viewer of the show. "It turned out really funny."

That's not the same reaction Richard and Mary Jane had when they saw their new "Slut Mobile." Tom had tricked them into lending him their car for an "emergency." He borrowed the car one afternoon, saying his was in the shop and that he had a lot of errands that needed to be done

ASAP. Mary Jane — perhaps foolishly — believed the sob story her son gave her and willingly handed over the keys. She was totally unaware of what he really had in mind for the car. "He had a key made and brought the car back and we didn't know," said Mary Jane, looking back on the saga, which turned out to be one of the best-known Tom Green skits. One night Tom waited until his parents were asleep, then he took the car out of the driveway to switch the hoods. At 3 a.m. he returned the car and sat in a refuse box at the side of his parents' driveway to wait for the sun to rise. "I think my parents really like lesbians, so to show my parents how much I love them I've turned their vehicle into more than just a vehicle. I've turned it into the Slut Mobile, he said. "Won't Mom and Dad be surprised and overwhelmed tomorrow morning when they get up to go to work?" Surprised is an understatement.

Dressed in a commando outfit, Tom had the cameras rolling at 5 a.m. as he crouched in his hiding spot. He didn't reveal his location until his father opened the front door and stood stupefied in front of his car. The look of shock on his face left no doubt about how he felt. "Holy Christ," he said, inspecting the picture with disgust. "Go talk to your mother," he added before he stormed off down the driveway. "What's the big deal?" Tom asked while chasing his father down the street. "It's completely untasteful and ridiculous," Richard said angrily to Tom, then told him to have the car painted back to its original condition — *immediately!*

Satisfied he'd bothered his dad enough for the moment, Tom rushed back home to see what his mother thought of the lovely portrait. Walking up the drive he chuckled to himself as he spied his mom scrubbing the hood of the car, desperately trying to erase the porno picture. Seeing her disruptive son coming up the drive, Mary Jane rushed back into the house and locked the front door. "It's not disgusting," Tom pleaded with her from outside. "Let me in the house. Let's talk." She was in no mood to be involved in any of his shameful exploits, which forced Tom to react in a bizarre fashion. He went off on a rant on how hard he worked on the project and how he just wanted to make everyone happy. "This is insane. I work so hard to make everyone happy. I hid in that box all night long and my mom has no intention of talking to me on camera about the Slut Mobile. Fortunately she left a few messages on my answering machine."

For the episode Tom used some creative camera tricks to show just how furious his mother was with the Slut Mobile. He split to a double shot on the television screen — one of the Slut Mobile, the other of Mary Jane with a dubbed voice-over of the messages she had left for him.

First beep: "Tom, it's your mother. Did you do that to our car? It's really gross and disgusting and I'm not impressed. I knew that something was happening. It's just another little horrible thing for us to cope with. Call me as soon as you get this message. I am livid."

Second beep: "Tom, this is your mother. That car better be back here immediately and put back to its original condition. And I don't find it funny. There's nothing funny about it at all. It's insulting. Once again it's not fun, it's ruining things that don't belong to you and it's making me sick and I'm fed up with it."

Third beep: "Tom it's 8 o'clock in the morning, you've been here and you've gone. I want my car fixed. It's disgusting."

Fourth beep: "Tom, it's your mother for the fourth call. I want the car taken and returned to its original condition or your dad and I are going to report this to the police. This is ridiculous, I'm not putting up with it. You can, you know, be charged with vandalism or whatever the charge would be. You're not going to ruin my things anymore and leave me in the lurch because I don't have a car to use. Now get over here and get the car and repair it immediately. And I'm not kidding."

Giving up on talking face-to-face with his mom, Tom decided to once again terrorize his father, who by this time was enjoying the peace and quiet of the bus stop with a half-dozen of his neighbors. Tom's philosophy on this: "Dad can't take the bus to work. I'm going to take the Slut Mobile to the bus stop." Driving up in the car he shouted out to his father, "C'mon, I'll drive you to work. Dad, don't worry if your neighbors see the Slut Mobile. It's just your Slut Mobile, right?"

The Slut Mobile was one of the worst pranks Tom has inflicted on the Greens. "It was so awful, although it was very well done, but the picture was rather graphic," said Mary Jane. "I'd just run into the house and lock the door saying, 'You're not coming in'" — a common reaction to the perils that she quickly learned came with the territory of giving birth to Tom.

✳

Aside from the occasional outburst, Tom has always had the utmost respect and concern for his parents, or at least that's what he wants his viewers to believe. That's what he set out to prove, anyway, when his mother was out of town on a business trip. Being a thoughtful son, Tom felt that his father would be lonely, so he looked to remedy the situation — at 3 a.m. "He came in the middle of the night with a bunch of dancing girls to entertain his dad," said Mary Jane. "I guess he thought his dad was pretty lonely and wanted to cheer him up." The girls, adequately dressed, turned on rock music and danced for Richard. When she heard about the dancing intruders, Mary Jane thought it was pretty funny. That was, until the same thing happened to her. Only this time Tom brought in a bagpipe player to serenade his mom to sleep. "He thought I had felt bad that I hadn't been similarly treated, so he brought in a highland dancer at 3 a.m.," she said. The only problem was that both parents were beginning to suffer from sleep deprivation because of his 3 a.m. visits. Both of them had to get up and go to work the following day. As it turned out, to Tom's chagrin, his parents were not as appreciative as he had anticipated.

Hoping to remedy the situation, he worked hard on a plan to make a better impression. Once again at 3 a.m. he invaded their bedroom, only this time it was to save their lives. Or so he thought. He had had a nightmare, or what he thought was a premonition, about an accident in his parents' bedroom. "I had a dream and I was thinking that maybe their bed was on fire," Tom said of his parents, cuddled up in their bed. "So I ran over here to save their lives." He arrived in their bedroom carrying a CO_2 fire extinguisher and opened fire on the nonexistent flames. There was nothing Richard or Mary Jane could do but huddle in their bed, shielding each other from the extinguisher residue and waiting for Tom to get bored and go home.

The next day, however, they were not as tolerant of his wild behavior and they responded in anger. His mother was furious and the first to yell at him. "Tom, that wasn't funny last night," she said harshly. "What you will come off as being is a grown-up brat." She was growing weary of dealing with his constant infringements on their peace and quiet and just wanted him to leave them alone for a little while. "Now I don't want you to do this anymore and I don't know how much clearer I can get," she told him. Even though he couldn't understand why his parents weren't thankful he had saved their lives, Tom was sure he'd done the right thing. "Next time there's a fire and I save your lives you won't be telling me to shut up, you'll be thanking your lucky stars you have a son like me who comes in the middle of the night to save your lives," he said on camera. "You'll be calling me a hero."

Not long after this incident, the Greens, frustrated and tired of his antics, were able to exact revenge on their out-of-control son. "We were able to get him back on his show and this time he was the one who got sprayed with the fire extinguishers," his dad said victoriously. They stormed onto the set of a *Tom Green Show* taping wearing face masks and carrying fire extinguishers, and hosed Glenn and Tom down. Even though the whole situation was choreographed, the Greens felt it was a small victory on their part. The audience was in hysterics as Tom lay in the slimy substance on the floor screaming, "Mommy, stop hurting me," while his father waved his hands in the air in mock celebration. After all the years of torment they had finally experienced the high their son felt in making a mockery of them and they were able to give him a little dose of his own medicine.

*

After the many years of enduring such Tom-foolery and mischief in their lives, the Greens began to get tired of falling asleep anxiously, knowing that their son might at any time burst into their dreams. They learned to sleep with one eye open for the better part of four long years. "It started out with little things and they gradually got bigger and bigger," Richard said, remarking that the worst pranks always occurred when Tom was living away from home. "He wouldn't come around for a while," said Mary Jane. "He'd let things cool off, then he'd come back and figure everything would be cool and we'd have forgotten about it." Fat chance. The truth was Richard and Mary Jane usually had a hard time forgiving him most of the time and were getting annoyed that Tom was spending the majority of his time harassing them. But to the

Greens' credit they rolled with the punches on camera and seemed to take the joking in stride . . . even if they were usually the victims.

In fact, after the first few pranks — "Plaid House" and "Slut Mobile" — they even began to relax a little. They realized that whatever Tom did to them he'd be responsible for the situation and would clean up the mess and, aside from initial embarrassment, it would be like the whole thing never even happened. So really they had nothing to worry about — aside from having their lives splattered on a nationally televised comedy show, that is. After the anger subsided they actually found the pranks kind of funny, and would admit that their lives were never dull. "It was funny because the whole time we were encouraging him to get a career and he was," Richard said jokingly while sitting at the breakfast table in their newly renovated kitchen (something they waited to do until Tom had moved out for good). "Only we would have rather he had a career doing something other than bothering us."

The Greens were skeptical of Tom's career choice and never expected that his show would succeed to the magnitude that it has. They felt he'd already missed his shot at fame. He had had a short-lived musical career and was nominated for a Juno Award. But still nothing had come of the experience. They put their faith wholeheartedly in Tom, hoping that his TV show would succeed. Their prayers were answered when MTV bought the show. Not only was their son gainfully employed, but he was also out of the country. For a little while they had a break from the constant glare of camera lights being flashed in their faces at all hours of the night. "I have to admit, when he calls I still look at the call display to see if it's an Ottawa area code or New York, just to be on the safe side," Mary Jane said.

Over the years the Greens got used to Tom's schedule. The only problem was they never knew what to expect. But they were beginning to see a trend in all the mayhem. They figured out that there was about a six-month gap between the major pranks he'd pull on them, giving them just enough time to relax, forgive him, and let their guard down before he'd unleash his turmoil once again. "We'd be in bed sleeping and as soon as we heard the dog barking and saw the lights coming down the hall we'd know," said Richard. "You'd say, 'Ahhh Christ, here he comes again.'" At one point they were becoming so frequent that one of Mary

Jane's sisters suggested Richard and Mary Jane go to bed in full makeup and wardrobe in preparation for an early-morning intrusion. "You know how cute you look at 3 a.m.," said Mary Jane. "Almost as great as when you come back from a 10-day canoe trip."

It didn't stop at makeup and wardrobe tips. The rest of the Green clan started to get in on the laughs too. Tom even used his grandmother for one skit, much to his parents' chagrin. During one Christmas break Derek and Tom set it up so that a briefcase of vibrators was left on his parents' kitchen counter. Acting upon urging from Tom, his sweet old grandmother, who was staying with them at the time, opened the brief-case. Totally unaware that they were sexual aids, she set out, with Tom, to find new uses for the devices. She used them as eggbeaters, held them up to her ears as a pair of dangling earrings, and Tom even went as far as to rub one on her lips as if applying a coat of lipstick. His mother was furious when she saw the footage of the afternoon Tom spent with his grandmother and did not wish to ever speak of the incident again.

This wasn't the only time Tom was the center of controversy in the Green home. Shortly after the show began, his parents realized he was using their house as his personal prop shop. The first item to go miss-ing was the beloved family portrait that hung on the living room wall, then tools and yard equipment would disappear without a trace. "He'd come and get everything from here," said Mary Jane. Richard quickly added, "It drove me absolutely crazy. We'd never have tools, or the snow shovel would be gone." After spending hours looking for lost items, the Greens would finally give up the search and face the facts — Tom had come shopping for set decorations and the chances of recovering the items were slim to none. Eventually they came to the conclusion he'd watched too much TV as a child. "I think he used to watch too much Mr. Dressup with his Tickle Trunk prop shop," his mother said with a smile.

Aside from their own humiliation and embarrassment the Greens feel that life with Tom has become somewhat normal. After all, they have been conditioned to his pranks since his childhood. People often ask them, "Why do you let him do it to you?" Mary Jane's answer is simple: "I'd like to send Tom to live at their houses for a while as their son." "It's not a question of letting him do it, there's not a whole lot of choice in the matter, really."

They have contemplated changing the locks on the doors on a number of occasions, but have always decided against it, thinking it would only be a waste of time. "He would find a way to get another [key] made anyway and then we would have just gone through a whole lot of nonsense for nothing," Mary Jane added.

After years of exploitation, Tom's parents have learned that it is easier to go with the flow than change his direction. Every time they even try to put a damper on his stunts he throws their words and actions right back at them. They have developed a thick skin and a penchant for the spotlight. For the Greens, living with Tom's pranks is a reality and, as they quickly discovered, it doesn't look like things are ever going to change anytime soon.

In fact, as it turns out, the situation could get very serious for them if Tom has anything to say about it. He confessed to *Entertainment Weekly*'s Kristen Baldwin that the ultimate prank he's dreamed of pulling on his parents would be to chloroform them and fly them off to Bangladesh. While they dozed he'd have their Beacon Hill home reconstructed on Bangladesh soil and then put them back into bed so that when they woke up it would be as if everything were normal — until they walked outside. Then, *bang*, they'd realize they were in another country.

Even if Tom is a safe distance away from Ottawa, the Greens should probably keep their suitcases packed, just in case!

8

DESTROYING THE EVIDENCE

Merilyn sank down in her seat and pulled her hands over her eyes, shielding her face both from the chaotic scene onstage and the debris flying through the air. She watched in horror as the set backdrops crashed to the ground and Tom and company rode from one end of the stage to the other on their skateboards, leaving a wake of destruction. As they careened around in front of the studio audience, tables were dismantled, chairs smashed, and the three basic walls housing the set were torn down and used as makeshift ramps for their jumps. She couldn't believe her eyes. They were ruining the set and they were not even done taping yet. There were still three episodes left before the season finale and she realized the show was in serious jeopardy — they no longer had a set and she had lost control. Brushing a tear from her cheek, she rose from her producer's seat at the back of the theater and walked swiftly out of the building without saying a word to anyone. "I was so upset that after the show when I usually hung out with the guys and said 'great show,' I decided to leave before the end." It wasn't until she was behind the wheel of her car that the *real* anxiety set in. She kept replaying in her mind the scene she'd just witnessed. "We don't have a lot of money to rebuild the set. What are we going to do?" she asked herself.

The question stayed fresh in her mind as she recalled an earlier conversation she'd had with Tom about the segment story lines and progression of the show. Knowing full well his penchant for destroying anything and everything in his path, Merilyn had sternly warned him of the financial restraints the show was under. "The deal is, Tom, you cannot destroy the set until the last episode because I don't have the money to rebuild it." Other than giving the gang the cold shoulder for a few days, however, there was little Merilyn could do to get her point across. Budgetary limits just weren't one of Tom's main concerns, especially when they came between him and having fun. He was in the "zone," scooting around the rubble to the cheers of his fans. He loved every minute of the mayhem. And it wasn't the first or last time he would let his destructive side have free rein.

During the first season on The Comedy Network, MTR decided to purchase suits for Tom's on-camera studio segments from Tip Top Tailors, but these met almost the same fate as the set. The handsome charcoal gray and navy suits, chosen in honor of Tom's hero, David Letterman, gave a classy feel to the show, allowing him to introduce each clip in style. But after the clips were through and the formal part of his talk show was over, Tom would lose the buttoned-down image and let his own quirky personality shine through. Each night after the show, Danielle Lacelle, production coordinator for *The Tom Green Show*, would be handed Tom's suits for dry cleaning. She never quite knew what to expect when they wound up in her arms. Sometimes hidden deep in the pockets and on the lapel she'd find dried whipped cream, caked on thick and crusty, while the sleeves would be so foul-smelling with the remnants of slimy fish that she was barely able to breathe when taking the clothes to the cleaners. "We dry-cleaned the clothes and everything but they had awful stuff on them. They wouldn't come completely clean," said Danielle.

During one season the running joke on the set was the disappearing prop desk. They had purchased the desk at a garage sale for $40. The gag was that each week Tom would fire up his gas-powered chainsaw, a prop he always kept close at hand, and carve off a section of the desk, to the sound of cheers from the delighted crowd. "You never really know what to expect when Tom Green is around," die-hard Green fan Sarah Jamison said with a chuckle. "If you were sitting in during the tapings of his show you quickly learned not to turn your attention away from him. It could lead to a very embarrassing situation for you." Faithful fans

Tom gets down and dirty with his favorite tool of destruction

knew what they were in for when they ventured to the show. There were times Tom and Glenn used the studio audience — outfitted in plastic sheets, goggles, and shower caps — to play a rousing game of "Human Xs and Os." During one show they smattered paint on the participants' heads, and during the finale for the 1998 season the cast rented a city bus and drove the entire audience home. Taking the joke one step further, Tom stumbled into their homes with them and went into the parents' bedrooms, waking them up just to say hi. He would rummage through their kitchens in search of food for the busload of travelers.

Whatever the gag, Tom loves including his audience. It not only gives him reassurance of their support, but they are often the inspiration for his work.

*

During the second season on The Comedy Network, Tom's growing fame was beginning to wreak havoc on filming street segments for the show. The attention Tom had always wanted was finally his, but at the same time it was seriously affecting his comedy, becoming a real problem. "We can't really shoot in Ottawa anymore because everybody recognizes us and it ruins it," Tom noted during an interview at MTR's offices in 1998. "It's at the point now where if we shoot in Ottawa nobody under the age of 30 is taken by surprise. Everybody pretty well knows."

Walking up and down Elgin and Bank streets in Ottawa, Tom's main quest was always to catch pedestrians off guard by making some very comical suggestions. People walking home from the office may have caught Tom wearing two bread sticks strapped to his head or dressed in full hockey gear and jumping into the Rideau Canal. It was becoming commonplace to see his antics on the streets and Ottawans were grow-ing conditioned to his behavior. Tom noted that "it was almost impos-sible for us to go do a bit on the street because people are like, 'It's Tom Green goofing off.'" Having people aware of what he was up to put a damper on the stunts and stripped away the part of the humor he was most fond of — people's reactions. "It changes the whole mood and vibe because I don't feel as comfortable doing it because people know the joke and then it's just not as funny," Tom complained, trying to deal with his increasing fame. Each time Tom, Derek, and Ray set out to film on the streets they would search out the people they thought would be the least familiar with the show. "A lot of older people don't know the show in Ottawa. I could go up to any 60-year-old woman in Ottawa and odds are she doesn't know who I am," Tom said. "But every 16-, 18- or 21-year-old that walked by while I'm interviewing her is going to be snickering, looking, and gawking and seeing what the goof-boy is up to. What's goof-boy doing with the old lady?" The reactions were draining for Tom as he fought to keep himself in character on the street. When people knew there was a joke coming it changed their reaction and his performance.

It was time to venture out of town again to get some new material, but this time instead of going south of the border, Tom and Derek decided to pack their bags and make the trek across Canada, spending the summer of 1998 exploring every crevice of the vast country. All they had left to figure out was how they were going to go about doing it. With limited resources they didn't have the cash to rent a car, and there wasn't enough space in their own vehicles, so they would have to borrow one. Their campaign to borrow a van, which they hoped would be a groovy old Winnebago decorated with peace signs, started by word of mouth through family and friends. When that didn't work, Glenn posted their request on *The Tom Green Show* website. To their amazement, fans from across the country sent in e-mails offering suggestions of places to stop along the trip and volunteering their parents' cars — without their permission of course. "We kind of did it just for a joke, not thinking anything would happen," Tom said. "But we started getting a lot of people who were offering us their campers from all across Canada." A bit surprised by the extreme generosity of their fans, Tom and Derek decided to borrow a blue van from 16-year-old Burlington native Sean Dickinson.

Sean's fascination with Tom Green had begun in early February of 1998, after a long week at high school. All Sean and his good friend Matt wanted to do the entire weekend was watch a little TV and relax. When the bell rang at 3 p.m. signaling the end of another week of tests and term papers, Sean and Matt headed over to Matt's house to unwind.

They spent the evening chatting with friends on the computer and later they turned on the TV. Thinking it was Saturday night, and being fans of *Mr. Show*, they were expecting to catch the latest installment of the comedy series. Turning the channel to The Comedy Network, Sean was mortified when he saw this weirdo being sprayed with a hose while wearing what looked like a turkey on his head. "This isn't *Mr. Show*," Sean exclaimed before quickly flipping the station. Realizing it was only Friday night, Matt chuckled when he saw Sean's reaction to the program. "I think that was *The Tom Green Show*. Flip it back," he said, asking Sean to give it a chance. Since it *was* Matt's house, Sean changed back to The Comedy Network and was soon mesmerized by the lunatic antics of Green as he frolicked around on the screen. Being an aspiring filmmaker himself, Sean was drawn to Tom's free spirit. He couldn't help but wish he had a show of his own like this. "I couldn't believe what this guy was doing," Sean said with disbelief. "He was doing all the things I always wanted to see someone do on TV, but I figured no one would ever let such a nutcase have a show."

Life, as Sean knew it, changed from that moment on. At the impressionable young age of 16, Sean soon found himself regularly surfing the Tom Green website and chatting with members of the cast, taping the show each week to replay with his friends, and meeting up with fellow Tom fans at a Toronto lounge appropriately called the Green Room. When he was feeling inspired he could be seen trying out some of his own skits in his hometown. "I ran around with a laundry basket on my head with 'Laundry Head' written across the top of the basket," Sean said, thinking back to unusual characters he had created. As Laundry Head he cruised around a Burlington mall interviewing stunned shoppers in Tom Green fashion. He received a back massage in a sexy lingerie shop and did the macarena with a young girl before security stepped in and questioned his sanity. Sean was certainly not insane; he actually used the stunt to help conquer his shyness. As he became more and more like the Tom Green persona, he began to feel more comfortable exposing his real self to the public.

By the time summer came around Sean was a full-blown Tom Green groupie. Every appearance in Burlington and the surrounding areas that Tom made, Sean was sure to be in the audience cheering his hero on.

At the same time Sean was becoming a fixture in the chat rooms, discussing with other fans segments they'd watched on the show. That was how he first saw Glenn's message requesting help in their search for a van to drive across Canada. "I didn't tell my mom but I sent them off an e-mail saying they could use my van," Sean said sheepishly. He thought he would never get a response back from the crew, but to his amazement, the next day he received correspondence from Derek asking questions about the van. It sounded like they really would like to borrow it.

"I figured then and there that I was going to have to tell my mom that he seriously wanted to borrow our van for six weeks to take across the country and do God knows what with," said Sean. He was a little afraid to tell his mother about the potential deal he had in the works for the family van his grandfather had bequeathed to him. "At the time my mom thought Tom was kind of a madman and she didn't like him much at all." Sean finally mustered up the courage to approach his mother

The road trip begins: "Old Blue" takes a large load
COURTESY SEAN DICKINSON

with the question and was relieved at her reaction. Although she was hesitant about lending their '86 Ford Econoline van to a bunch of strangers, Elaine couldn't help but admire her son's dedication to his favorite TV show. "Sean has always wanted to write movies," she boasted. "I wanted to give him a little break to see what it was like." With her blessing Tom, Derek, and Ray were awarded summer custody of "Old Blue" with one small stipulation built into the agreement: Sean would accompany them on the first few days of the road trip.

When Sean found out, he was going on the road trip it felt like he had won the lottery. Just imagine — he was about to spend three days with his heroes and find out what it was really like to make a TV show. The departure date was set for June 28 and Sean could hardly contain his excitement. Tom Green was actually coming to his house!

Still suffering pangs of shyness, Sean devised a plan to make himself feel more secure when the trio arrived. He wanted to be fully prepared so he wouldn't be caught off guard. Setting his alarm for 8:30 that morning, he woke up early to shower and pack, and then decided to grab a quick nap before they arrived to pick up the van. As soon as Sean's head hit the fluffy pillows on the couch he drifted off to sleep. He looked so comfortable that when his mom went in to ask him to move the van out to the front of their house she couldn't bring herself to wake him. He was curled up in a little ball at the end of the couch, so she decided to let him get a few hours' sleep. He probably wasn't going to get much rest on the trip.

She stepped outside to move the van herself. "Good morning," a voice called out to her from the curb "We're looking for Sean and Elaine Dickinson's home." Walking towards the figure she introduced herself and said, "You must be Tom Green. Sean is sleeping on the couch inside. I'll go get him." Tom had a better idea. Grabbing Ray and the video camera, the two walked into the Dickinsons' living room and roused Sean from dreamland. Startled and still half-asleep, Sean wasn't quite sure what was happening when he woke up. There were bright lights, a huge camera shoved in front of his face, and this wacky-looking guy trying to interview him. "I wasn't sure for a few minutes what the hell was going on because it all seemed so surreal," he confessed of his first meeting with his TV idol. "I thought I might still be dreaming."

As Tom gyrated across the room, Sean's sleepy-eyed spell was broken and he realized *Tom Green* was in his house and the trip was about to begin. Walking downstairs to say good-bye to his mom, Sean met up with Derek in the kitchen. He introduced himself and Derek began joking with him right away, asking Sean how he felt about going away with three gay pedophiles when they were all going to be sharing one sleeping bag. The nervous tension surrounding the group of strangers dissipated and Sean broke into a fit of laughter as he demonstrated the self-defense techniques he had learned as a green belt in karate. Nobody was going to be messing with him! Packing up Old Blue, Sean gave his mom a quick kiss on the cheek, hopped into the back of the van, and waved as they pulled away from the curb.

Looking around the truck Sean couldn't help but smile. This was it. He would be spending the next three days with Tom Green, learning from behind the scenes how to make a TV show. Life just didn't get any better than this.

✱

Being out on the open road rejuvenated Tom and Derek's creative energies. There was something new to see each time they looked out the window, and they had the freedom to spontaneously stop and film whenever they discovered something they thought could be included in a segment. A big part of their show had been the insanity they discovered in their everyday lives and in improvising their way in and out of some sticky situations. During the first season Derek and Tom had traveled to Kingston and on their way home came across a car impoundment lot. They worked it into a skit about Derek trying to break in to retrieve his lost automobile. "If we'd have been on Elgin Street we wouldn't have thought of that because we wouldn't have been near a car compound," Tom said, referring to the skit where Derek was caught by the guard as he tried to scale the fence. "Driving across the country there are new landscapes and new things that we'll see that we've never seen before that all of a sudden an idea would come from," Tom said with excitement. "We'd be driving along the highway and there would be a dead moose on the side of the road, which we wouldn't see if we were in

Ottawa. So we'd get out and I'd hump the dead moose until a construction worker pulled over and told me to stop, you know. We'd film that and it was really kind of weird and then we'd move on."

Although it was a road trip and the sights were often synonymous with their locations, Tom, Derek, and Ray worked hard to conceal their change of venue. "The reason we went on the road trip was not because we wanted to make, like, a big road-trip show," Tom explained after returning from their six-week adventure. "You'd watch the whole season and you'll never know we were on a road trip. We're not saying, 'OK, now we're here in Kenora, Ontario, and this is how wacky it is in Kenora.'" They wanted the comedy to be the focus, not the locations they visited. It was more important to reveal the universal weirdness exhibited by the people in each new town. Once, while driving along the highway, they spotted an oil derrick with flames shooting 300 feet into the air, so they stopped to chat with the workers monitoring the blaze. "We'd go up and knock on the door with the construction workers and try and get them to audition for a movie," Tom said, reliving the scene. "We had this weird thing we shot with them with this surreal background."

Making stops in small communities off the beaten path, they'd pick up the local newspaper and search for inspiration. They were hunting for stories that were odd or strange, and if they couldn't find something outrageous they often came up with their own leads. For example, while driving, Derek made a point of noting that there was an unusually large amount of mutilated roadkill along the highway. That discovery led the group to St. Paul, Alberta, where they located an expert in the field of cattle mutilation. The expert, taking their questions seriously, led them out into a deserted pasture to witness his findings. "He thought the aliens in St. Paul were coming down and killing all the cattle," Tom said with a snicker. "This guy is an expert who works in the field of cow mutilation and he truly believes the aliens come down and kill the cattle." Tom, Ray, and Derek made the trek out into the middle of the field and saw first-hand the rotting carcasses scattered in the field. They couldn't help but laugh at the reasons the "expert" was citing. After picking up a few examples of the mutilated animals and getting the scene on film, the group packed up their video equipment and headed back out on the

Tom is ready for the citizens of North Bay, Canada. But are they ready for him?
COURTESY SEAN DICKINSON

road. They were eager to see how the highway roadkill looked compared to what they'd witnessed in the fields.

The trip wasn't just about roadkill though. The most memorable part of the journey was the amazing way they experienced the countryside. "We would drive 20 km one day. You know, we'd drive up the road, we'd be in Medicine Hat, Alberta, then we'd drive two hours to Swift Current and stay in Swift Current, Saskatchewan, for two days. We'd walk around, we'd look, we'd talk to people, we'd go investigate and look into stuff," Tom said, describing their adventures. "We'd know all the nooks and crannies; we wouldn't just fly through Saskatchewan. We spent like four

Just a little male bonding

or five days in what normally takes five hours to drive across. We really got a good feel for being Canadian and it was kind of neat," Tom remarked. "You always wonder what's out there, but to actually go and live in these provinces for a few days or weeks, to go and spend a lot of time in Northern British Columbia, to look around and not feel worried about having to get somewhere."

The only itinerary the group had was to follow the map route Derek had created in order to coordinate accommodations with Danielle back in the office. She would call motels a day ahead of them and try to finagle free rooms in exchange for credit on the show. She also set up publicity along the way; one such stop occurred at the Calgary news station CFCN where Tom appeared on the *News at Noon* broadcast. "I knew he was a bit of a prankster, but I had no idea what I was in for," remarked Michelle Gayse, the journalist interviewing Tom. "He took control from the moment he arrived at the studio." Michelle tried her hand at interviewing Tom during the second-last segment of the broadcast. "He was very unpredictable," she said, joking that he hijacked the interview. "We were lucky that we introduced him at the end of the show otherwise we might have had some problems because during the last segment we usually promo the harder news stories." Tom had smothered his entire head in a foamy layer of shaving cream and danced across the stage behind the two female co-anchors while they tried to maintain their composure and report the day's news. "Just when I thought there was a way to tame him, he'd lose control," Michelle said.

✻

During the first three days of the trip, while Sean was on board, the group managed to stay out of any serious trouble. Aside from some minor pranks, like outsmarting some Canadian Tire service-station workers in order to zoom around the garage on a mechanic's bench, Tom spent the better part of Sean's trip trying to find him a date. In North Bay, Ontario, he strutted around town getting advice on "how to pick up chicks" from the locals before seeing Sean safely to the bus depot. Boarding the bus, Sean was sad that his adventure was over. So Tom followed him into the bus to send him off in true Green style. "He said good-bye to everyone on the bus and told them to look after me," said Sean, recalling the moment fondly. As the bus rolled into motion, Sean looked out the window and blew a mock kiss in Tom's direction which was returned in kind. "Then I apologized to the people up front for Tom running around and kissing them," said Sean, who noted that his fellow passengers on the bus were a bunch of fun-loving folks. "They all laughed and said it was OK."

The bus trip was exhausting and by the time Sean returned home he was delirious with excitement. He had just spent time on the road with his hero, Tom Green. With a roll of photos for his scrapbook and

memories that would last a lifetime, Sean spent the next few weeks
sharing the stories with his friends and other Tom Green fans, who
didn't believe he had actually gone on the trip. Eventually life got back
to normal for the teen, but it didn't last long. One afternoon in August,
when Sean was sitting at home working on his computer, the phone
rang. It was a long-distance call from the RCMP inquiring about a blue
Econoline van. Old Blue had been pulled over. Concerned citizens had
phoned in a tip to police that a suspicious-looking van had been driving
slowly around their neighborhood. When the van was pulled over, Tom,
Ray, and Derek tried to explain how they were just filming a television
show. The police officers laughed at their story and, after checking their
driver's licenses and the van's registration, were convinced that the van
was stolen. They were under the impression that Tom and company
were thieves casing the houses in the neighborhood. Adamantly deny-
ing they were part of a burglary ring and reiterating that they'd borrowed
the van from a friend, the group pleaded with the officers to give them
the benefit of the doubt. The officers agreed to check out their far-
fetched story and placed a call to the Dickinson home in Burlington.
"Apparently Tom was in a ski mask going around a community in
the van filming people at night," said Sean. "I guess people got scared
and phoned the police." Once Sean cleared up the confusion and the
police were convinced Tom, Derek, and Ray weren't a threat, the group
ventured back on the road.

They decided to play it safe for a while and made some unexpected
detours for what they affectionately call "prop stops." Tom and Derek
were always on the lookout for obscure items they could use on the show
to create intrigue for their viewers. Items such as the beloved "Poetry
Shovel" and the mascot "Racky the Raccoon" took audiences by surprise
when Tom used them in some very unpredictable circumstances. Most
of their prop stops happened on the side of the road where they would
come upon garage sales. They would pick up old and discarded items
for a few dollars. On their way to North Bay the group had stopped at a
yard sale full of hidden treasures; spending under five dollars, Tom
picked out an old wig and a pair of flaming red earmuffs, both from the
1980s. Sporting the new look, Tom walked along the neighboring streets
getting a few sideways glances from the residents.

One of the best prop stops was made by accident when they were cruising through Lillooet, BC, and stopped at a gas station to refuel. When Derek went inside the booth to pay, he stumbled upon an interesting-looking item that he'd never seen before — an electric flyswatter. The prop had great potential for use on the show, but Derek left the store forgetting to purchase the eccentric contraption. An hour down the road he brought up the subject of the flyswatter. "We've got to have that for the show," Tom said excitedly before making a quick pit stop to phone the office. "Danielle, you have got to get this flyswatter for me," she recalled Tom begging. "It's really important, it could make or break the segment," Tom pleaded with her over the line. Luckily they had kept the receipt from the gas station. He gave Danielle the name and phone number to call and have the flyswatter mailed back to the office. "The store attendant was a little confused when I called him requesting the item but he sent it back to Ottawa for the show," said Danielle. "He didn't really understand what we wanted to use the flyswatter for on the comedy show. He didn't really see the humor in the everyday item." Tom and Derek saw this item as a prop gem that they could use for most of the next season. Once they knew it would be safely stored along with dozens of other props back at the office, they continued on with their journey.

With thousands of kilometers clocked on Old Blue, the van held up surprisingly well. It had overheated once and a tire had been punctured driving over a nail in Thunder Bay, but it wasn't until the group maneuvered their way through the Rockies that things got a little sticky. With all the twists and turns on the mountainous roadways, the brakes were fried by the time they got to BC. Taking a few days off to relax and get the van back into drivable condition for the return trip to Ottawa, Tom decided to check in with MTR and find out what was happening back in the city. What he didn't realize was that things were really heating up back home, and one of the biggest opportunities of his career to that point was coming to a head. Merilyn informed him over the phone that the office had received a call from Bruce McCulloch of *Kids in the Hall* about a movie he wanted Tom to audition for. A few days later Tom was temporarily abandoning the road trip and boarding a plane back to Toronto to work on his Hollywood feature-film debut.

*

Tom was more than thrilled just to have been asked to audition for a part in *Superstar*. It was like a dream for him to work alongside some of his peers for a film that was being produced by the creative sketch-comedy offices of *Saturday Night Live*. Landing back in Toronto, the first thing he wanted was some downtime to go over the script and relax. He called MTR's Toronto producer, Steve Jarosz, desperately pleading to crash on his couch for a few days. "He was nervous and wanted to go over his lines right away," Steve said, punctuating the fact that Tom was taking the audition very seriously. Getting comfortable in Steve's rec room, Tom talked the producer into going through the lines with him so he could get into the role. The scene they rehearsed took place in the main character, Mary's, apartment. Tom had to put the moves on her. "He was sitting on the couch and he was supposed to be getting me sexually aroused, but I couldn't get into it so I called for my wife," Steve laughed. "It was incredible; his character brings over a CD, *Green-Eyed Lady*, puts on the music, and Tom goes into this erratic dance trying to turn her on." Tom's mating ritual lasted more than an hour and a half as he gyrated around their home exclaiming, "I'm going to rock your world!"

The following morning, Tom was prepared for the audition and psyched about the chance to meet some of his comedic heroes. He hailed a cab and was shuttled off to the tryout to strut his stuff. It wasn't until two weeks later, while Tom was back into production for *The Tom Green Show*, that the producers from *Superstar* came calling. "He didn't get the part that he read for. Instead they cast him in a smaller role, but liked him so much they kept writing more scenes for him," said Steve. "And he was worried he'd blown the audition by being too over-the-top."

Soon enough Tom found himself hanging out on the set with comedians Will Ferrell and Mark McKinney — a far cry from the company he usually kept. Getting accustomed to the Hollywood hoopla was a little disconcerting for Tom. It wasn't like his own show where he was surrounded by his close friends and spending the day goofing off in front of the camera. He had lines to memorize and marks to hit. This was a big deal. "It was such a surreal experience hanging out with these people," Tom said. "I respect them all and they've always been big influences on me." A little nervous about the star power of the film, he took a breather and headed off to Steve Jarosz's house to run through his lines a few times before the cameras were set to roll. Although he didn't have much to say in the film, he wanted his part to be perfect.

Superstar is centered around the tenacious Mary Katherine Gallagher, the hygienically challenged character Molly Shannon brings to life on *SNL*. You might remember her as the one dressed in a Catholic schoolgirl's uniform running around the stage sticking her fingers in odorous body parts and then smelling the stench. Ewww, gross! Tom was cast — without much of a stretch — as the wisecracking sidekick to Ferrell's character. To get into character, Tom said he was told to be as outgoing and loud as possible. "I'm the obnoxious kid who doesn't like Mary Katherine and thinks she's going nowhere," he said in character while spouting off one of his lines: "You SUCK!!!"

His nerves aside, acting had become second nature to Tom. Having logged hundreds of hours in the editing suites and in front of the camera, he was becoming a seasoned pro. After all, *Superstar* wasn't his first film experience. He had a bit part in the low-budget film *Clutch* and in August of 1997 he had been asked by Ottawa filmmaker Susan Terrill to appear in a cameo role for her short film *The Chicken Tree*. Written by Toronto writer Jamie Zeppa, the 15-minute short was adapted for the screen by scriptwriter Sara Snow for entry in the Canadian National Screen Institute where a handful of filmmakers from across Canada are chosen each year to develop a short film. Given an infusion of cash and film stock, each team brings its compelling story to life.

For Terrill the picture was a labor of love. Shot in Quebec and Lanark, the film depicts the life of a young boy (David Deveau) searching for meaning in his life and something to call his own. The majority of the film was shot in a small cottage where the boy, separated from the world, spends time with his neurotic mother (Nancy Beatty). While his mother passes her days complaining about the unsuitable conditions of their abode and the noisiness of the neighborhood children, the boy watches the kids. He is jealous of their laughter and carefree spirit. In one scene the young boy boards a city bus and has a conversation with the bus driver, convincing him to make an unofficial stop. The bus driver was played by Tom Green. "It was really entertaining to have him in the film," says director/producer Terrill. "He was given lines, but of course he improvised and it was very funny."

With the growing success of *The Tom Green Show*, the doors slowly began to open up for Tom. He was gaining valuable experience in acting, directing, editing, and production. He was meeting some very influential people that could help him achieve his goals. Tom Green the character was becoming a recognizable figure and it was time to capitalize on his success. Merilyn Read was ready to set her plan in motion.

9

THE BIG APPLE
TURNS GREEN

With *The Tom Green Show*, MTR and The Comedy Network had created a program that was competitive in the Canadian market and successful at capturing more than 40,000 fans per week. Tom Green had acquired a cult following across Canada and, after years of hard work and dedication, it was time to take it to the next level. MTR decided to take advantage of the growing audience base and youthful energy of the show and move it to a bigger platform. The staff behind MTR's production machine worked feverishly from their Ottawa offices setting up screenings of the show for major American networks. It was during this period that Merilyn recalls receiving what she calls, "one of the most significant phone calls in the development of the show." She was going over some contracts late one evening at home when the phone rang with a Los Angeles number. She picked up the receiver and said hello. "Merilyn Read," said the voice at the other end, "this is Cori Stern. I'm a producer with Fox Family. Can I talk to you a moment?" Although taken a bit off guard with the late hour, Merilyn was intrigued. "Sure," she said putting her feet up on the coffee table in front of her. "What's up?" Bubbling over with enthusiasm, Cori began telling Merilyn how she'd gotten hold of a few sample tapes of The Tom Green Show and how much she loved the program's clever undertones. She wanted to present it to the executives at the Fox Family Channel, who are known for their drive to provide viewers with family-friendly entertainment. Merilyn felt flattered as she hung up the phone and immediately sent 13 episodes to Cori in Los Angeles for review.

Cori was interested in possibly purchasing segments of the man-on-the-street clips from the show to be used as entertaining filler between their regularly scheduled tween/teen-oriented programming. Watching the segments carefully, Cori kept in mind the channel's mandate: entertainment that was edgier than Nickolodeon, but not as out there as MTV. "We knew some of Tom's stuff would work great for the saavier teens and draw a lot of attention, but some of it would be too much for our audience," Cori wrote, citing Tom's infamous Grandma bit as an example of the latter. She made a note of the time codes for each of the segments she thought would mix well with their current programming, and sent the codes along with the tapes off to the pur Standards and Practices Department at Fox Family for approval. "Somehow the note didn't make it to them," she explained. "They received the tapes, reviewed all the segments and called me in a panic, thinking I wanted to put the shows on the air in their entirety." After clearing up the misunderstanding, Cori tried to sell the segments to the channel, but ultimately Fox Family decided that it wasn't the time to put the Tom Green Show on their air. For Tom and Merilyn this was a blessing in disguise. There was a much bigger deal in store for them. Cori still saw potential in the show and asked for Merilyn's permission to send the tapes out to a few of her contacts in the industry, one of whom was John Miller at MTV. It was October of 1998, and the hard work of MTR and Tom Green's crew was about to finally pay off — big time!

Seated in her Ottawa office, Merilyn received a call from Miller in New York. He was on his way out of the country but was eager to talk with her about Tom's show. "We don't want the show as it is," his voice crackled through the bad reception of the cellular phone. "I don't like the show as it is. I'm not willing to buy the show as it is," he said before the cell transmission was abruptly cut off. For Merilyn this was the negative response she had been hoping and praying to avoid. Fully aware of Tom's determination to keep the creative content of the show intact, she knew he'd never agree, for whatever sum of money, to change the elements of his program.

Comedy Central had also shown interest in the show, so she never returned Miller's call. A few weeks later, however, Comedy Central passed on *The Tom Green Show,* saying it was too young for their demographic. Merilyn was worried about the future of the show until she received another call from Miller. His voice boomed over the line. "Why didn't you call me back? I want the show," he said to her amazement. She shot back with her tough-as-nails attitude, "You said you didn't want it as is." But for Miller it was only a case of making a few minor adjustments. He was hungry for the show and wanted to make it slicker with less time between jokes. He felt it needed a little reworking and re-editing, but that was all. His enthusiasm for moving the show to the MTV studios in New York was apparent from the jovial tone of his voice. And, to be honest, everyone felt that MTV was the most suitable match for Tom's unpredictable sense of humor. Merilyn was in complete disbelief as she hung up. "This is big, this is major," she repeated to herself over and over before picking up the phone once again, this time to call Tom and share the mind-blowing news with him. MTV wanted him immediately and asked him to hop a plane to California to pitch the show to the network executives.

The growth of the show from this point on was solely on Tom's shoulders. It would be up to him to wow the bigwigs at the audition and secure his self-titled show a U.S. network deal for the spring of the following year. That meant only one thing — the performance of his life. Tom took the meeting with the network very seriously. He had come a long way and paid his dues — working for free for most of his career — and now it was time to taste real success. This was his chance to make it and he wasn't about to let it slip away.

Dressed in a suitable jacket and tie, he sauntered into the intimidating LA boardroom full of programming execs and commandeered their attention with a compilation tape of 10 solid minutes of *The Tom Green Show.* He answered, with sincerity, their series of questions about the history and future of the show. "I was pretty serious about it ... I wanted to show them that I was actually a sane person," Tom told Tony Atherton of the *Ottawa Citizen* after he made the pitch. "I basically went in and told them about the show and all the elements and why it would be good, and played some clips [including one of Tom sucking on a cow's teat]. I think that counterbalanced my seriousness."

If that wasn't enough to pique the interest of John Miller, MTV's senior vice-president of programming, what happened next most certainly clinched the deal. After the formal presentation Tom amazed the room by giving them a real-life Tom Greening. He smothered his tall, lanky body with a rich, foamy layer of shaving cream and, looking like the aftermath of someone caught in a barbershop explosion, dove onto the large oak desk in the middle of the room. With his arms flailing and cream spewing, he screamed nonsense at the high-powered captive audience. It's nice to know that some things never change. The MTV deal was sealed with a contract for 10 repackaged shows using MTR segments made in Canada with an option to commission 13 new ones and acquire the rights for the show from MTR.

It was with bittersweet feelings that *The Tom Green Show* crew rolled into the Arts Court Theater for the final taping of the Ottawa segments in November of 1998. The crew, who had worked so closely together on a common project, were witnessing the end of an era, and it was with heavy hearts that they said their good-byes. The sense of independence and renegade humor that the show was founded on was in total control of the set — audience, artists, and crew. Nothing would hold them back. And as Merilyn and Tom stood outside the Arts Court Theater for one last run-through, she took him aside and said, "Just take a whiff, Tom. That's the smell of freedom. You'll never again have this experience of total freedom."

Bursting through the barriers of television comedy and bounding into the absurd, the show was completely out of control. There were cell phones being stuffed in dead raccoons and dead raccoons being sawed in half. The audience was being sprayed down with hoses. The last Ottawa episode was complete anarchy and the crew loved every minute of it. It was all done in the name of freedom.

Shortly after the Christmas holiday Tom and Derek made their exodus from Ottawa to the bright lights of New York. Packing only essentials from their Ottawa apartments, the pair made their way across the border to take up temporary residence in a posh Manhattan hotel. Tom was still in disbelief at the quick turn of events that was the cause of this pivotal transition. "It's all so crazy," he kept repeating to family and friends who called to wish him well in his new digs. But crazy had nothing to do with it — outside of his lunatic stunts, that is. The move to New York was a very calculated step. Tom had been surrounded by powerful people who believed in his talents and it was his time now. He was about to become a star. MTV was ready to induct a new renegade prankster to taunt and tease the *South Park* generation of television viewers.

✷

New York City is incredibly beautiful under a veil of darkness. The large neon billboards surrounding Times Square come alive with their advertisements, enticing people into the downtown core. It wasn't the excitement of the city, however, that held my attention during a trip to the Big Apple in January of 1999. It was an Ottawa comedian. I was sent by the *Ottawa Sun* to interview Tom Green, about to become MTV's newest sensation. Arriving in New York, I didn't expect to see beat cops pausing for a photo with tourists or an elderly grandmother casually pushing a stroller through Central Park. Where were all the gangs, the crime, the fear?

"The city is so different now from when I spent a summer here 10 years ago," Tom said, echoing my feelings as he looked down from the second-story MTV studio he called home. "I was afraid when I came down 42nd Street back then. It was really scary and I was 17 at the time." Tom was referring to the time in his career when he was a part of the rap band Organized Rhyme and the group had ventured to New York to record a music video. During that time New York's downtown core was overridden with crime and violence, giving tourists a very bleak image of the city and Green a longing for home. Ten years later Tom was back and the drastic change in the city's atmosphere was one that instantly set his heart at ease. He didn't have to be fearful of being mugged while skateboarding around town or through the cordoned-off areas at the Empire State building; all he had to worry about now was security guards keeping up with his tricks.

"It feels so much friendlier now," he remarked. "Kind of like home, only more traffic." But even with the pleasant surroundings of the city, feelings of melancholy for his suburban Ottawa home haunted the 27-year-old talk-show host. "I'm homesick," he said, with pangs of loneliness apparent in his voice as he looked around the trendy MTV studio for something, *anything*, that was familiar. His eyes locked on his loyal friends Glenn, Phil, and Derek. Out of allegiance to their buddy Tom, Glenn and Phil decided to fly in for the weekend tapings, taking a break from their day jobs. Derek relocated to New York to retain his position as segment writer.

In mid-January of 1999 the production staff at MTV, close to 35 strong — a real difference from the volunteer staff at Rogers — started the first rehearsals and tapings of the Americanized *Tom Green Show*. While the format remained the same for the half-hour-long program — Phil sitting in the window behind Tom's desk sipping gallon upon gallon of coffee, Glenn on the couch as the guinea pig for Tom's schoolboy pranks, and Derek behind the scenes writing the same comedy that the group grew up on — there were some modern conveniences added to give the show a slicker appearance. One of the biggest changes for both Derek and Tom was the induction of eight writers, flown in from across the U.S. to aid in scriptwriting. "It's so much easier now," Tom acknowledged after taping wrapped for the second show of the day. Although he still felt responsible for whether the show would succeed or not, it gave him some peace of mind knowing that he had more help and time to prepare the show. Both Derek and Tom admitted they were beginning to feel the burn of constantly having to come up with new segment ideas for the Canadian series. "There was a lot of pressure before because it was just Derek, myself, and Ray who were out going across the country, and for eight weeks we'd have to think of everything."

The relief of new reinforcements in the writing department allowed everyone time to focus and offer their best work. With new people joining the ranks, MTV wanted to be sure everyone on board understood the brand of humor behind Tom and the show. The result was a huge Tom Green marathon for the benefit of the new writers. "Everyone here knows the style of the stuff I'm doing because the writers have watched hundreds and hundreds of tapes and hours and hours of *The Tom Green Show*," explained the host. "It makes it a lot easier than if they were coming on fresh."

In just a few short months things had changed drastically for Tom. The show went from a bare-bones production where the crew would spend power weekends hammering out 12 studio shows in two days in the Ottawa Arts Court Theater to a slick, semi-polished production created by the finest equipment and staff available. Their schedule became a lot less cumbersome. Waking at around 11 a.m. every day, Tom, Derek, and the writers would spend a week working on one show, which was then taped before two separate studio audiences to ensure optimum laughter.

"With the small team before, we just didn't have the ability to have everything scripted," Tom said. The improvement in the flow of the program was instantaneous. Instead of memorizing his lines and jumping around frantically when he ran out of material, as in the first few seasons, he graduated to having a slew of script assistants and staff to make the process run smoothly. "As soon as we sit down and change an idea, the next second it's typed up and five minutes later it's on the TelePrompTer," he said with amazement. That's another new addition to the set that he had to get quickly acquainted with. The first time he used the prompters, placed on the floor and on one of the cameras, was during a dress rehearsal, and he was admittedly a little confused. He stumbled while trying to jump, mid-sentence, from one prompter to the other, but 15 minutes later his composure was restored. He got right back into his regular shtick, which included warming up the studio audience by shoveling a handful of live earthworms into his mouth. Typical Green appeal. It helped that a few of the audience members were fans of the Canadian show. They had ventured to New York to help their favorite comedic idol get adjusted to his new surroundings. "It was so comforting to see familiar faces in the audience and it helps that they were Ottawa-pride guys too," said Derek. "It helped put things into perspective." The studio fans helped to get the ball rolling by shouting out familiar pranks to their host, getting him into character.

But it wasn't just the familiar faces that made the new studio feel like home — it was Tom himself. He managed to get both staff and fans past those first few awkward moments when the whole scenario of their show debuting on MTV seemed all too unreal. "Eww, look at the dirt and saliva dripping from his tongue," one audience member squealed at Tom as one of the worms escaped from his grasp and wriggled around the marble-like floor. Tom was in his natural element.

Despite his penchant for creepy-crawly worms, his U.S. show seemed tamer to audiences accustomed to the raunchy and at times shocking material on The Comedy Network. Tom has repeatedly said that he does not want to be known as a "shock comic." His goal is to entertain his fans and create humor that makes people laugh and think at the same time. He wasn't worried that some die-hard fans think his show has lost its edginess. He felt that Canadian audiences had the opportunity to be conditioned to his brazen sense of humor and he was just giving American audiences the same respect.

MTV agreed wholeheartedly with the scaled-back nature of the show, and was counting on the longevity of the program. After all, it was the off-the-wall comedy, not the grotesque stunts, that first captured John Miller's attention. Miller was relying on Tom's uniqueness, irreverence, and underlying intelligence to entice imaginative and impressionable young minds to the channel — something MTV programming has been doing since its inception.

"I wouldn't exactly say his humor's subtle, but there is definitely some wittiness and cleverness to Tom's brand of comedy," John said after the show's second week of tapings. Miller recognized that he'd more likely than not be pushed to the borders by Tom's outlandish stunts, but his main focus was to guide Tom in different directions too. "I think our roles are to challenge each other. I challenge Tom to do his brand of comedy within a structure so that it actually has a larger impact," he said confidently. However, he is the first to admit that Tom's instincts are to be completely random and fly off the wall at will. "He'll push to do whatever the hell he wants without having any sort of setup or context or payoff. I'm constantly riding him to make sure it does have those things and still maintains an irreverence — a freshness and uniqueness. And Tom is going to push me not to have gray hair by the time I'm 35."

John is certain that while the show continues to grow and develop, Tom will constantly be pushing the envelope where creativity is concerned and political correctness is on the line. "I think he'll really make sure that it's always as edgy and clever as it can be. But I'm challenging him to always be clever instead of constantly going for the big crazy joke right out of the gate."

✳

It was well after midnight when the crew wrapped up taping of its third episode. As the clean-up crew worked hastily to gather up any remaining worm parts still loose on the floor, Tom and his new production team gathered backstage in the Green Room to praise each other on a job well-done. Much like the rest of the MTV studios, the Green Room is trendy and funky. The soft lighting flickers off the turquoise-colored walls and illuminates the oversized chairs and couches. Tom bounced into the room looking a little harried by the week-long creative process, but in good spirits as he launched into stories of his latest brush with fame. "We all got to meet Wayne Gretzky and we even got signed sticks from him," said an enthusiastic Tom as he recounted meeting the Great One at an NHL game. He explained how Gretzky came up after a hockey game and chatted with the group about life in the Big Apple and their new MTV show. The week before, former Ottawa Senators hockey player Stan Neckar had showed up to watch a rehearsal for *The Tom Green Show.* "I guess he's a big fan of the show," gushed Tom. "Afterwards he came back to the Green Room and invited us all to a Rangers game. It was the best." Tom felt as though he was in heaven, and it was sure looking that way. After all, it was just a few short years earlier that Tom and crew were putting in 90-hour work weeks to produce the show. Now there were assistants, directors, and production aids at his beck and call.

"Mr. Green, would you like that delivered to your room?"

"Mr. Green, here's your press call for tomorrow."

"Mr. Green, is there anything else you require?"

Tom seemed a little uncomfortable with all the attention focused directly on him. Although he certainly was used to being the center of attention when it came to his pranks, in day-to-day life he was not used to all the fuss. A production assistant knocked quietly on the Green Room door and Tom's attention was torn from his conversation about Gretzky to a new pair of sneakers she was holding in her hand. "These were sent over for you, Mr. Green," she said with a flirtatious giggle in her voice. "Shall I send them over to your hotel room?" "Yes," Tom politely answered as the group headed out of the studios into the main reception area. The scattering of 20-something staffers once again loitering around the halls remarked how funny Tom was, and how terrific the taping went — quite the ego boost. The group moved towards the large double oak doors that act as a barrier between the trendy underworld of the studio and the hallway that opens to the outside world. On the other side of the doors, two security guards patrolled the entrance. The crew poured out of the studio, down the endlessly churning escalators, and out to the street. Derek, Tom, Phil, and Glenn stepped out into the crisp mid-January evening.

They were greeted by a small group of fans waiting outside for the chance to talk with Tom. As always, he was ready, willing, and able to impress. "You were amazing," one fan called out to him. "That was the best shit I've seen in a long time," said another. Getting his second wind from their encouragement, Tom launched into an impromptu skit on the street that involved jumping into a half-full garbage can on the corner. It only took a few minutes before a small crowd had gathered around Tom and their infectious laughter spread down the street, drawing more and more curious passers-by — including two police cruisers. "He's got a banana peel on his head. He's crazy," said visiting Toronto native Don McNabb, pointing to Tom and laughing hysterically. After a small production number Tom reluctantly stepped out of the trash bin and bid farewell to the enormous crowd.

The group continued down the road to a local tavern they frequent to hold after-hours meetings. A few rounds of milky White Russians went down smoothly and the team got comfortably seated in the cozy couch and wingback chairs in the small conversation area at the front of the bar. Glenn, Derek, Tom, and Phil broke the ice by throwing out a few vulgar topics for debate, including one of their favorites — masturbation. The conversation turned very graphic very quickly as a debate over different techniques became the focal point used to engage people entering the bar in their sordid conversations. Receiving the reaction they were looking for — mostly disbelief and embarrassment by other patrons of the tavern — another raucous debate began regarding the actual height of the stack of dirty laundry piling up in Tom's bedroom. "I'll just wait until my underwear is all soiled and then I'll run out and get some new stuff," Tom said sheepishly. "Laundry is not my thing."

Keep New York City Clean
Don't Litter
Put It Here

✳

Just a few short months before he moved to New York, arranging interviews with Mr. Green simply meant picking up the phone and organizing a time and location with his Ottawa production staff. But being part
of the U.S. entertainment industry has been a different experience for
Tom, who had always taken a hands-on approach when it came to media
coverage of his career. Suddenly he is no longer personally reachable by
phone and virtually inaccessible through the MTV PR offices. He has
been swallowed whole by the multiple layers of MTV staff, who are very
selective as to who gains access to Tom. It is up to the PR staffers to
decide which newspapers or TV interviews will be acceptable for Mr.
Green's new image. The group is small and controlled by MTV. During
the first few rehearsals and tapings in New York, press was excluded
from viewing the studio segments and given the runaround when
scheduled interviews were to take place. Some phone calls requesting
interviews were returned with nasty messages containing remarks about
how insignificant some reporters were to the development of Mr.
Green's career. Suddenly, members of the Canadian press who had
helped nurture that career were left out in the cold.

To their credit, however, the network is sinking a lot of money into
The Tom Green Show and is most certainly looking for big results. They
aren't willing to take any chances. Almost immediately after signing the
contract with MTV, full-page ads appeared in *Entertainment Weekly* and
Rolling Stone magazines, bombarding U.S. audiences with their first
glimpse of Tom Green. It was a clever ad campaign designed to captivate
audiences and draw their attention to the show before any episodes had
even aired. The campaign was a success. American media response to
the show was extremely positive.

"It's a brand of nose-thumbing that combines insurrectionist tendencies with a twisted interest in repelling the very audience it attracts,"
wrote Paula Span of the *Washington Post*. "Tom is a master at creating
screwy comedy by thrusting himself and innocent bystanders into absurd situations," Kristen Baldwin of *Entertainment Weekly* proclaimed.
"Green's Letterman-without-personal-boundaries shtick can captivate

like a train wreck and is almost always amusing," announced *Rolling Stone*'s Mark Healy.

By the second week on the air in the States *The Tom Green Show* had captured the American cable market with a stronghold on the MTV 12-to-34-year-old demographic. Plus they were running a close second behind MTV's other hit program, *Celebrity Deathmatch*, in the 18-to-24-year-old viewer market. The U.S. debut of *The Tom Green Show* reported astronomical numbers of more than one million viewers weekly. Not bad for a little cable show from Ottawa.

✷

David Letterman is not just a talk-show host; to Tom Green, Letterman is an idol. He was the inspiration for Tom back in high school when the youth first started getting ideas for his own comedy show. He emulated Letterman right down to the tennis sneakers and suit jacket he wore when Derek filmed their make-believe talk show. Just a few short months after arriving in New York City, Tom Green was close to coming face-to-face with Letterman as a guest on *The Late Show*. MTV had sent tapes over to *The Late Show* and there was a lot of interest, especially in the man-on-the-street segments. Back home, Green's Ottawa production team was duly excited with the publicity going into the MTV show and were thrilled when they found out Tom was scheduled to sub on *The Late Show* after a last-minute guest cancellation. Unfortunately, shortly after Green received word that the interview was a go, the guest rebooked and his late-night appearance was put on hold. But MTV didn't give up and a few short weeks later he was given the Green light, so to speak.

Shuttled the three short blocks from his Manhattan office to the Ed Sullivan Theater in a luxurious black stretch limousine, Tom was more than a little bit nervous. He even went so far as to ask the driver to circle the block a few times. It was with that shy, star-struck sweetness that Tom appeared on *The Late Show,* stupefying his hard-core fans by contradicting his on-air persona. There was nary a can of shaving cream or a dead animal in sight. Tom strolled out onto the stage with a silent confidence, taking the seat beside his mentor without hesitation, but also without incident. In fact, it was Letterman who initiated the first comical debate after Tom set up a clip too early. "I just don't want to screw this up," Tom confessed after Letterman threw a few friendly shots in his direction.

But the real sparks flew after Tom introduced his beloved "Slut Mobile" clip. We are all familiar with this prank by now — it's the one where Tom had the pornographic image of two lesbians air-brushed on the hood of his parents' car. Even though the stunt did not get initial laughs from Tom's parents, it did get a laugh out of Letterman, who confessed that the videographer-style clips he had worked on in the past were tossed from *The Late Show* after a number of disturbing incidents. "Somebody was nearly killed one too many times," Letterman said half-jokingly on the show. "After a while people in New York City don't think your little game is all that funny."

The Letterman show was just the first step in a roller-coaster ride of television appearances, interviews, and advertising. MTV wanted Tom's image everywhere. It was his second television appearance that allowed fans a glimpse of the real Tom Green in his natural element. For more than a decade the perky morning duo of Regis and Kathie Lee have been entertaining viewers with their wake-up program. In mid-March the MTV mega-media machine went back to work and Tom soon enough found his way onto the morning talk show. This time his hard-core fans were not disappointed. He ambled onto the set wearing what looked like a metallic blue storm-trooper uniform and carrying a white plastic baton that he kept beating over his own head. During the interview he repeatedly slipped off his perch, falling onto the floor amid laughter from the studio audience. Tom was in control. He managed to coax Regis to use the baton to strike his bottom while Green yelled, "Regis, hit my bum-bum. Regis, hit my bum-bum." Green's reputation had definitely preceded him as Regis and guest host Bernadette Peters, filling in for Kathie Lee, immediately began asking him about all the weird things he'd done to his parents and why. "They are nice people too," Philbin said to Tom during the interview. "They look like a God-fearing couple."

The stunts Tom has performed on his parents are legendary. They are also one of the major reasons why he was asked to appear on the Oprah

Winfrey show. But he did not venture there alone. He was reunited with his parents for a special Mother's Day program featuring guests who have pledged to give up habits their mothers hate. Well, Mrs. Green has a few habits she'd love Tom to lose. Perhaps he could stop painting their house plaid while they are away on vacation, or refrain from plunking dead cow's heads on their bed in the middle of the night, or possibly not paint pornographic images on the family car. Those were just a few suggestions. But when those quintessential parental figures, Richard and Mary Jane Green, appeared on Oprah's show it was quite obvious they were waiting for yet another punch line from their son.

"I have a feeling there's something coming after," Richard admitted on the show, while Mary Jane confessed that the only reason she attended the interview was to meet the queen of talk, Oprah Winfrey. Tom got the last laugh on his parents once again. After snapping a quick photo of the patient couple with Oprah, he announced that he loved them both very much and was sending them on a spectacular 12-day cruise through the South Pacific to Tahiti. Not a bad installment in the payback he owed his parents for the years they were unwillingly the butt of most of his jokes. Quite aware of Tom's track record, his parents learned over the years to be suspicious of their son's seemingly sweet behavior, and as they walked off the stage they were still waiting for the punch line. Luckily for the Greens, for the moment it seems Tom has outgrown his parental hijinks phase. His time and energy have been diverted to new pranks that have taken him across the States — although this time it was not for his show but as the new spokesperson for a low-calorie soft drink, Pepsi One, which hit the market in October of 1998.

The soft-drink giant capitalized on the buzz surrounding *The Tom Green Show*. Putting more than one million dollars into the advertising campaign, Pepsi One sent Tom on a U.S. road trip. He drove cross-country in the convertible Pepsi-mobile filled to the brim with samples of the soft drink during the 1999 Final Four NCAA basketball tournament. He was spotted at universities in Arizona, Cincinnati, Maryland, and Tampa. He was doing what he does best — making normal, everyday people question reality and, at some point, their own senses. Within the series of 10 commercials, Tom took over a classroom as Professor Green teaching Pepsi 101, judged a soft-drink–chugging contest, held a taste test with Pepsi One against a glass of water containing a goldfish — no goldfish were harmed in the making of the commercial — all while screeching into a megaphone taunting students to take a taste of the new drink. Out of fear or curiosity, some sampled the drink through some unconventional means — drinking it out of their winter gloves, lapping it up off their hands, or lying down on the ground and having Green pour the soft drink down their throats.

So why did Pepsi One take a chance on Tom's off-the-wall sense of humor? Pepsi believed the match was perfect. Tom's fresh and youthful approach to entertaining complemented their objective of offering an alternative soft drink to diet-conscious consumers. "Tom has a way of connecting with people in a very powerful and effective way," said Jon Harris, senior manager of public relations for Pepsi One in Purchase, New York. "He's very funny and willing to take risks."

For Tom Green that is surely an understatement. In the few short months since he'd arrived in New York, Tom had become the talk of the town and learned to create a frenzy wherever he ventured. All of his dreams were coming true. All that was left was to sit back and enjoy the ride — and what a wild ride it turned out to be.

✳

Tom has engineered several clever events in his career, but none more successful than when he managed to string along both his fans and the media in February of 2000.

Arriving in Ottawa for the weekend, Tom brought with him a very special companion. Not only was she the hot topic of conversation around water coolers everywhere, but she also outweighed Tom in the controversy category: her name was Monica Lewinsky. And from the moment they arrived in town, people began to talk. The pair were sighted all over the city and the question being asked was: is it the real Monica Lewinsky? It was debated over lunch, argued over drinks and discussed in the media as reporters tried frantically to confirm the young woman's identity.

The question was put to rest when the high-profile couple made their first television appearance. Anna Podrebarac, producer of the Ottawa version of *Daytime* (an information and entertainment program on Rogers cable), was sitting in the Richmond Road studios on Tuesday, February 8th. She was spending the afternoon preparing for the next day's show when she received a phone call from Tom's writing partner Derek Harvie: "He said Tom was coming to town in a few days and he'd like to appear on the show," Anna said. "Derek also said he (Tom) would be bringing an 'A' list celebrity with him." As Anna hung up the phone she immediately started thinking. What is Tom up to?

All too familiar with his stunts on other TV show, she knew that this wouldn't be a calm interview. "Derek assured me that nothing crazy was going to happen," she said. "But I persisted, saying, 'Could you give me an inkling of what you have planned, just in case the director needs to change the camera shots?'"

But Derek's lips were sealed, and for the most part Anna took his word that the show would remain respectable. "Tom's known for bringing a dead raccoon's head on the Mike Bullard show," she said skeptically. "And I was a little afraid that something like that would happen."

Setting her concerns aside, Anna spent the next few days trying to keep Tom's arrival a secret. "It was very hush, hush," she said. "The only person I let know in advance was Jon Dore, one of the show's hosts. I knew he'd have to prepare for the interview and didn't want to just surprise him the day he (Tom) arrived."

Calling Jon into her office on Wednesday, Anna filled him in on all the details she was privy to, but it wasn't until later that evening that she found out the identity of the mystery guest. Once she knew Monica Lewinsky was coming to town she took it upon herself to track Jon down to give him the news. "Being a comedian and having some Monica jokes in my routine I guess Anna wanted me to know ahead of time," Jon said.

The excitement didn't set in until he got to the studios the next morning. Arriving shortly after 10 a.m., he noticed a difference in attitude among the mostly volunteer staff.

"There was quite a buzz and everyone was really excited," he recalled, admitting to feeling pangs of nervousness himself. "I was definitely excited, but in my mind Tom was bringing two other friends with him on the trip — paranoia and suspicion. I had no idea what he would do."

For Jon, preparing for the interview was the easy part. The hard part was swallowing the reality that he was about to become part of one of Toms P.R. stunts. As the interview began on live television at noon, those feelings were solidified.

"I asked him why he was back in town, and he answered that it was for a major announcement the following day," Jon said laughing. "And the first thing I thought was that he was go to say he was joining Jenny Craig."

After about 15 minutes of gentle banter between Tom and Jon, with a polite Monica giggling in the background, the pair departed. This is when the rumors began. They ranged from people speculating that the pair was going to announce a wedding engagement to others claiming Monica was bearing Tom's child.

A short 24-hours later the mystery was solved. After struggling up the ladder to the roof of the Little Beaver Restaurant in Vanier, Tom walked up to the microphone and looked out into the sea of fans and media that had gathered for the bizarre news conference. Encouraged by the chanting crowd and the glare of the lights from the TV cameras, Tom began his mock conference. He declared Ottawa the fabric capital of Canada, and the perfect place for him to help friend Monica Lewinsky launch her new line of handbags.

"For the past three days and nights Monica Lewinsky and I have scoured this city looking for the perfect fabric, for a perfect new handbag," Tom said. "How did we find the best fabrics in the world? We came to Ottawa. We searched every nook and cranny of this town and we left no stone unturned, no nook uncrannied."

Once the crowd realized there was no "real announcement" and that this so-called news conference was just another episode from the weird world of Tom Green, he called Monica up onto the roof. Ridiculed for her indiscretions with the president of the United States, Monica found support from the Ottawa crowd who shouted positive remarks her way. "We love you Monica," one fan screamed. "Will you marry me?" yelled another.

Looking demure and shy, Ms. Lewinsky simply stood beside the flamboyant Green and smiled. Tom held up a handbag from Monica's line and began to explain the story of its construction. "After scouring the

Tom and Monica do Ottawa

fabric shops all around this city, Monica and I were able to make this handbag from the cloth of my parents' bedspread, which we procured two nights ago at 4:00 in the morning," Tom said before holding the bag up for the hoard of photographers.

After 30 minutes of joking with the crowd, Tom gathered his friends Phil Giroux, Glenn Humplik, and Monica Lewinsky and left the building. His fans and the media were left trying to digest what had just happened.

A few days later everything fell into place. Tom was gathering footage to use on his MTV show in the U.S. Excerpts were shown on *Entertainment Tonight* and Tom joked about the way reporters intrude into the lives of celebrities: "The funny thing is that we're making fun of them," he said during the MTV segment. Tom was aiming the spotlight straight back on the media, and giving them a small, bitter taste of how public personalities feel about their intrusions.

10

BACK TO THE BASICS

This is The Tom Green Show.
It's not The Green Tom Show.
This is my favorite show,
Because it is my show.
If this was your show,
You'd probably like it more
Than I did.
That's because it was your show,
But it's not your show,
It's The Tom Green Show.
— Theme song from *The Tom Green Show*

By the time Tom Green finished warbling his way through his silly theme song on-air for the first time, television broadcasting had changed. *The Tom Green Show* was different; it was raw and imperfect, but filled with a seemingly endless supply of energy and creativity. It was, as the theme song so emphatically claims, *Tom's* show. And Tom was a different breed of animal. He was refreshingly courageous about defying the conventions of talk television and he displayed a prodigious imagination. He could relate to his viewers because he was a viewer himself.

David Letterman has long been his inspiration, so Tom modeled his self-titled television program after his idol's late-night talk show — with a few enhancements. The basic format, an extension of the host's character, has remained consistent: an off-the-cuff mock studio interview intertwined with a bohemian style of videography. Since the show's inception in 1994, the mechanics have stayed true to the original format with only a few minor exceptions. When it first went on the air it was a monster of a program; the original format was an hour-long broadcast. The outcome was inevitable — quantity took precedence over quality. When The Comedy Network picked up the show two years later the result was a streamlined half-hour program. The shorter length enabled the cast to work on fine-tuning the look of the show and allowed them more time to polish the comedy segments. The change was a success, making *The Tom Green Show* a more marketable program. The show was so well received that MTV picked up the show for their spring 1999 schedule, thus launching Tom's career.

When *The Tom Green Show* debuted on MTV in January of 1999, die-hard Canadian fans were surprised by the obvious changes to the dynamic of the show. The Americanized version appeared glitzier and more clever; it almost seemed like mainstream television. By the time the Comedy Network shows had wrapped up taping in Ottawa, the subject matter had gotten so out of control and grotesque that it could have been considered borderline offensive to viewers. When it resurfaced in New York, the cast had regained their composure and the show went back to the basics. The opening theme song remains, with some slight alterations. Opting for a cleaner look, the old opening sequence, featuring Tom dancing around with a dead chicken on his head, was ditched in favor of a tighter version. The MTV opening features Tom outfitted in a lab coat and sporting a pair of oversized clear plastic goggles that secure two flapping feather dusters over his ears — typical Tom Green. As for the set, it has retained its art deco feel. As always it remains unobtrusive, giving viewers the impression that its components have just been purchased at a garage sale. The old backdrop, which Tom and company hand-painted, was discarded for a more glamorous multicolored stained-glass-window effect.

As for the cast, a sharply suited Tom Green sits idly behind the interview desk poking fun at cohost Glenn Humplik. For his part, Glenn is unscathed by the MTV transition and remains completely unaware of his surroundings. As always he dresses himself in casual attire, giving the

The boys toast their Big Apple arrival

audience the impression he's just stumbled into the studio after sleeping in late. And the chortling Phil Giroux, who made his big break on the show by being one of the irrelevant background events Tom chooses to ignore, still peers through the window behind Tom's desk, giggling at inopportune moments throughout the show. His coffee-swigging gig has gotten cushier, however; MTV splurged and purchased a chair for him to sit on.

One of the most visible changes MTV made after purchasing the show was to rework the studio interview portion. What was to Canadian audiences the most volatile segment on the show quickly became the most entertaining. With the help of writers flown in from across the U.S., the show's dialogue was tweaked for optimum laughter and Tom's interview style has followed suit. The ever-present possibility of surprise and danger that lurked in every unscripted moment for Canadian audiences has been replaced with witty banter, and the addition of a punchier, well-scripted chitchat between Tom and Glenn designed to provide an underlying sense of stability. Not only does the show look more professional, but the host seems more in control and comfortable with his subdued character. Perhaps the calmer version of Tom Green is in part due to the fact that he is still surrounded by his core group of friends, which for the most part has remained constant throughout the development of the show.

For MTV the focus has shifted slightly from the outrageous studio bits Tom used to perform to better-choreographed video clips. At first the video segments were comprised mostly of Tom's best clips from Rogers and The Comedy Network. U.S. audiences were enticed to watch the show by the promos hyping the "Buying Condoms" clip and the introduction to Tom's parents in the "Slut Mobile" footage. In fact, for MTV, the street segments have begun to bear a resemblance to those taped while the crew was working as volunteers on Rogers. The subject matter is tamer and focuses more on comedy than shocking. Tom has been allowed the opportunity to get back to what he enjoys — physical humor.

One of the most popular segments on *The Tom Green Show*, the pranks he inflicts on his loving parents, was incorporated into the MTV version. Richard and Mary Jane Green, who quickly became famous themselves, continue to be the butt of Tom's jokes, even tough he resides in another country. During the summer of 1999, Tom returned home to Ottawa for a mini-vacation and turned it into a business trip. Falling back into his old routine of embarrassing his parents, Tom and the MTV crew erected life-size statues of the Greens on the front lawn of their home. The statues, supposedly bearing a likeness to his parents, were placed in a very compromising position for the viewing pleasure of the entire neighborhood. By the time Richard and Mary Jane made their way out of the house to see what their offspring had done, they were horrified by the scene. To show his adamant disapproval, Tom's dad knocked down the figures and scolded his son for the immature stunt, all of which was caught on tape — proving that some things will never change.

During the time *The Tom Green Show* was backed by The Comedy Network, the group had been given wide latitude with respect to the creativity of the show. Shaving off corners of his desk or microwaving a dead raccoon were part of the controversial charm of the program. During the transition to include U.S. audiences, the creativity level of the shows has taken a huge step backwards as Tom and Derek work to condition American audiences to their special brand of humor. They want to ease into the irreverence so as not to scare off potential fans.

It appears that Tom is trying to discard the "shock" label he inherited from Canadian journalists by revisiting some of his more demure and clever stunts. For the benefit of American fans, Tom has acted like a corpse outside a fruit stand and mocked pedestrians with the aid of a police radio. Although this piece is quite funny, it is incredibly tame compared to what his longtime fans are accustomed to witnessing. Tom has abandoned his trademark grotesque stunts in favor of more cleverly scripted jokes. For example, on the MTV version of the show, Tom has drawn attention to himself by portraying an allergy sufferer held captive inside a huge clear plastic baseball rolling around a ball diamond and interrupting a game. He has also posed as an elderly shopper scooting around a grocery store driving a motorized cart, banging into shelves and knocking down items piled neatly in the aisles. While other customers in the store stood dumbfounded by the scene, store clerks were furious with Green's antics. "Get out of the store," they demanded. "You're going to have to leave!"

As it turns out, Tom's attempts at shucking off the "shock" label may have been short-lived after all. A want-ad of sorts was posted on MTV's Tom Green website requesting pregnant women to contact the network if they wished for Tom to appear at the hospital during the birth of the child. It seems that Tom was once again treading in familiar territory for his second season on the barrier-pushing network.

Looking back at the debut of *The Tom Green Show* on Rogers, many things have changed for the cast and crew. One of the first stunts Tom performed that night was to dump a bag of kitty litter on his head. The gag nearly suffocated him as the fumes left him gasping for air. On MTV you wouldn't see a stunt so out of control. On the surface it appears the show has lost a bit of its edge in the transition to the U.S. It doesn't seem so dangerous anymore. The anarchy and chaos the show once thrived on seem to have been lost in the shuffle. Perhaps the host has grown out of his "prankster" behavior and is ready to try his hand at mainstream television.

CONCLUSION

Just like the skittish albino guinea pig, Skinny, who found a vegetable paradise in the delicacy-laden playground of Tom's desk, Tom himself found a kind of heaven in New York and Los Angeles. At 27 years of age he was living his dream. His new office in the 32-story Manhattan MTV office building was just a few blocks from the Ed Sullivan Theater, the place where his idol David Letterman hangs his hat. Tom was ecstatic. "I just can't believe this is all happening," he exclaimed over the phone to me. "It's so crazy." At that moment life was perfect. At last he had everything he wanted and all the frustrating setbacks he'd experienced finally seemed worthwhile. But things were about to get better. After only six months in the U.S., Tom gave American audiences a true Greening when MTV released its first set of ratings for the show. The numbers were strong and growing, predicting what Canadian fans had already known — *The Tom Green Show* was a hit. After all, over one million American viewers couldn't all be wrong.

With the television universe seemingly conquered at last, Tom was ready for more. Derek Harvie, who worked behind the scenes as head writer for the show, was already on his way. In the summer of 1999 his name appeared on *Entertainment Weekly*'s "It List" as one of the 100 most creative people in entertainment. He was in good standing alongside Heather Graham, Nicole Kidman, Fatboy Slim, Rupert Everett, and company. Then, a few weeks after Derek's bit of good fortune, Tom signed a lucrative deal with Touchstone Pictures, a division of the Walt

Disney Co., to write and star in his own movies. Tom had hit the big time. The years of goofing around, embarrassing himself, and working for free were finally paying off.

In the late 1990s movies and television programs took a drastic change in direction. The momentum shifted from targeting shows at older audiences to redirecting the product towards the younger generation. A number of programs popped up that aimed their structure at a specific demographic — teens and 20-somethings. The result was a slew of shows such as *Dawson's Creek, Buffy the Vampire Slayer, That '70s Show* and *Party of Five.* They explored younger concerns, from dating and homework to starting college and getting married. The dialogue was frank and refreshing and blew open the doors on what conventional broadcasters considered entertainment. They made way for programming that was barrier-pushing in content, and vulgar and irreverent subject matter soon found its way into mainstream television. A stream of programs like *Duckman* and *South Park* appeared, expanding on this theory and introducing the viewers to what is playfully termed toilet humor. The more outrageous and disgusting the joke, the bigger the laughs.

With "in-yer-face" entertainment at the forefront, the timing was perfect for *The Tom Green Show* to move into the market. Not only was the show fresh and unique, but it also appealed to the right crowd — Gen X and Gen Y and their no-holds-barred attitude. *Tom Green* was exactly what they wanted: realistic programming that dared to delve into society's fascination with the grotesque.

As I see it, *The Tom Green Show* is a version of *Candid Camera* for the new millennium. Tom is fascinated by people's reactions to bizarre situations and has taken on the irreverent project of eliciting those responses with zeal. And the oddball way he torments both strangers and his parents connects him with fans who live vicariously through his exploits. Although every time his parents complained that his "hobby" of having a television show was interfering in their lives, he responded with bigger and more annoying stunts, they have always tolerated his pranks and nurtured his growth. They aren't alone. Tom Green has a long list of supporters who have helped and encouraged him to pursue his dream. Without Merilyn Read, Ray Skaff, and Ed Robinson in his corner Tom may never have found the success he enjoys. But along with the joys of being a parental figure to Tom come certain perils, as Richard and Mary Jane Green will attest.

Comedian/talk-show host Mike Bullard best summed up his ambivalent affection: "Tom Green is the son I would have chopped off my penis to avoid having."

WORKS CONSULTED

Atherton, Tony. "Cable cult star Tom Green gets local CBC show." *Ottawa Citizen.* 11 August 1995.

———. "Green subdued, funnier in MTV debut." *Ottawa Citizen.* 27 January 1999.

———. "He's Ottawa's very own TV oddball." *Ottawa Citizen.* 11 February 1995.

———. "Hog wild." *Ottawa Citizen.* 27 October 1996.

———. "Ottawa comedian gets US talk show." *Ottawa Citizen.* 5 January 1999.

———. "Please, Tom, do it for mom." *Ottawa Citizen.* 4 May 1999.

———. "Tom's most excellent adventure." *Ottawa Citizen.* 4 February 1999.

Baldwin, Kristen. "Green grosser." *Entertainment Weekly.* 12 March 1999.

Barker, Jeremy. "Pranks get the Green light." *Ottawa Citizen.* 13 July 1999.

Beat Factory. Organized Rhyme publicity. A & M Records. 5 December 1991.

Berry, Ivan. Interview with the author. 20 August 1999.

Bickley, Claire. "Comic has host feeling Green." *Toronto Sun.* 24 November 1998.

Bullard, Mike. Interview with the author. 14 June 1999.

Campbell, Elaine. Interview with the author. 13 July 1999.

Campbell, Greg. Interview with the author. 7 September 1999.

Campbell, Hugh. Interview with the author. 6 July 1999.

Canadian Press. "Celine Dion sweeps Juno nominations." *Ottawa Citizen.* 9 February 1993.

———. "Hairy ending for Tom Green season." *Ottawa Sun.* 1 May 1998.

———. "Ottawa's own Green takes aim at movies." *Ottawa Sun.* 18 August 1999.

Cavanagh, Trevor. Interview with the author. 26 September 1999.

Cavanagh, Trevor, Darcy De Toni, and Tom Green. "Proposal for *The Tom Green Show.*" 15 April 1996.

Century, Douglas. "A prankster as a model of decorum." *New York Times.* 28 February 1999.

Colonel By High School yearbook. 1988.

Cook, Tim. Interview with the author. 3 September 1999.

CRTC. "CRTC Decision 96-596." Online. 4 September 1996.

Cuddy, Don. Interview with the author. 13 July 1999.

De Toni, Darcy. Interview with the author. 17 July 1999. e3

Dickinson, Sean. Interview with the author. 13 July 1999.

Fitzgerald, Dez. Interview with the author. 16 June 1999.

Foster, Dean. Interview with the author. 28 June 1999.

Foster, Peter. Interview with the author. 6 November 1999.

Gaudreau, Shirley. Interview with the author. 8 June 1999.

Giroux, Phil. Interview with the author. 24 January 1999.

Gorman, Brian. "How a little talk show got a national audience." *Ottawa Sun.* 22 July 1997.

Green, Mary Jane. Interviews with the author. 19 November 1998; 19 March 1999.

Green, Richard. Interviews with the author. 19 November 1998; 23 February 1999; 19 March 1999.

Green, Tom. Interviews with the author. 27 May 1998; 21 September 1998; 19 january 1999; 24 January 1999.

Grignon, Denis. "Playing for laughs." Newspaper article included in MTR Entertainment's press kit for *The Tom Green Show*, newspaper and date unavailable.

Harris, Jon. Interview with the author. 10 June 1999.

Harvie, Derek. Interview with the author. 24 January 1999.

Hawkins, Shannon. "Big Apple about to go Green." *Ottawa Sun.* 20 January 1999.

———. "Big Apple turns Green." *Ottawa Sun.* 31 January 1999.

———. "Green and bear it all." *Ottawa Sun.* 28 April 1999.

———. "Green comedian hits big time." *Ottawa Sun.* 24 February 1999.

———. "Green meets idol David Letterman." *Ottawa Sun.* 26 February 1999.

———. "Green takes it national." *Ottawa Sun.* 27 May 1998.

———. "Green takes on daytime talk." *Ottawa Sun.* 24 March 1999.

———. "Tom foolery." *Ottawa Sun.* 30 September 1998.

Healy, Mark. "*Tom Green Show.*" *Rolling Stone.* 1 April 1999.

Humplik, Glenn. Interview with the author. 24 January 1999.

"'It' List." *Entertainment Weekly.* Online. 25 June 1999.

Jarosz, Steve. Interviews with the author. 14 July 1999; 24 August 1999.

Juno Awards. Online.

Klymkiw, Slawko. Interview with the author. 23 August 1999.

Lacelle, Danielle. Interview with the author. 24 June 1999.

Leroux, Jacki. "New *Grey Owl* takes wing." *Ottawa Sun.* 9 May 1998.

Lewer, Ian. Interview with the author. 3 September 1999.

Lisle, Lisa. "Green's antics have firefighters seeing red." *Ottawa Sun.* 15 April 1999.

Lofaro, Tony. "Ottawa comedians laugh it up on Regis and Kathie Lee." *Ottawa Citizen*. 24 March 1999.

——. "Wacky comic, king of pop." *Ottawa Citizen*. 12 March 1999.

MacLean, Kerry. Interview with the author. 7 June 1999.

McHarg, Karen. Interview with the author. 12 August 1999.

Miller, John. Interview with the author. 24 January 1999.

MTV.com. Online.

Mullington, Chris. Interview with the author. 9 July 1999.

Peacock, Leisa. Interview with the author. 2 November 1999.

Pearce, Tralee. "Everything's gone Green." *Ottawa Sun*. 10 February 1998.

——. "Greening of Mexico." *Ottawa Sun*. 27 November 1997.

——. "Greening of the CBC." *Ottawa Sun*. 29 October 1996.

——. "Looking at the world through Green-colored glasses." *Ottawa Sun*. 28 April 1996.

——. "*Tom Green Show*." *The Ottawa Sun*. 7 November 1996.

Pickles, Karen. Interview with the author. 15 August 1999.

Posner, Michael. "The lady and the gross-out king." *Globe and Mail*. 30 September 1999.

Pressman, Allan. Interview with the author. 20 July 1999.

Read, Merilyn. Interviews with the author. 21 September 1998; 24 January 1999; 24 June 1999.

Robinson, Ed. Interview with the author. 18 June 1999.

Rockburn, Ken. Interviews with the author. 8 July 1999; 20 July 1999.

Shulgan, Christopher. "Tom does his parents proud . . . this time." *Ottawa Citizen*. 8 May 1999.

Skaff, Ray. Interview with the author. 22 June 1999.

Slotek, Jim. "Pepsi generation looking Green." *Ottawa Sun*. 11 March 1999.

Span, Paula. "MTV's offbeat comedian." *Washington Post*. 9 March 1999.

Stackpole, Mickey. Interview with the author. 28 June 1999.

Stewart, Tom, Interview with the author. 12 August 1999

Stone, Jay. "Behind Pierce Brosnan." *Ottawa Citizen*. 22 September 1999.

——. "Tom Green is wild on screen." *Ottawa Citizen*. 29 October 1998.

Thorn, Ian. Interview with the author. 3 September 1999.

Thorn, Wayne. Interview with the author. 7 June 1999.

Tomgreen.com. Online.

Vegas, Johnny. Interview with the author. 8 September 1999.

Wagman, Howard. Interview with the author. 14 September 1999.

Whyte, Murray. "The color of funny." *Details*. May 1999.

Wrona, Stephanie. "He's Green but he's learning quickly." *Ottawa Sun*. 26 March 1998.

CHRONOLOGY

1971 Born in Pembroke, Ontario on July 30 to Richard and Mary Jane Green. Spends his childhood in Ottawa attending Robert Hopkins Public School, Henry Munro Middle School, and Colonel By High School.

1983 Wins Grade Six speech competition.

1990 Tom Green, Greg Campbell, and Geordie Ferguson form the rap group Organized Rhyme.
Tom and Greg are asked to host the CHUO (Ottawa University Radio Station) rap show.

1991 Tom and Greg enrol in the Algonquin College broadcasting course.
Organized Rhyme starts performing live at Ottawa bars.
Organized Rhyme taken to New York City to produce their first video.
Tom drops out of broadcasting program.
Organized Rhyme is asked to be the opening act for the Dream Warriors in Halifax.

1992 Organized Rhyme signs with the Boombastic label under Beat Factory on A&M Records.
Organized Rhyme releases their first album, *Huh!? Stiffenin' Against the Wall*, and their first single, "Check the OR."
Organized Rhyme signs on as spokespersons for Loeb pizza.
Organized Rhyme nominated for a Juno Award for their single "Check the OR."

1993 Organized Rhyme attends Juno ceremony on March 21, 1993, at the O'Keefe Centre in Toronto, but loses to "Keep it Slammin'" by Devon.

Organized Rhyme splits up.
Tom reapplies to Algonquin College broadcasting course.

1994 Tom, Trevor Cavanagh, and Darcy De Toni write the initial proposal for *The Tom Green Show*.
First season of *The Tom Green Show* on Rogers Community TV.

1995 CBC gives *The Tom Green Show* a production deal for a network pilot in June.
CBC pilot falls apart due to creative conflicts in August.
Second season of *The Tom Green Show* kicks off with a broadcast from the Central Canada Exhibition (the Ex) in September.

1996 Merilyn Read comes on board and renews the CBC pilot deal.
The Tom Green Show pilot airs on CBC across Ontario on October 31.

1997 The Comedy Network launches commissioned episodes of *The Tom Green Show* on October 17.
Tom films small part in Canadian film, *The Chicken Tree* in August.

1998 *The Tom Green Show* debuts on The Comedy Network on February 13.
Tom appears in the *National Enquirer* for smooching Pierce Brosnan on the cheek during his filming of *Grey Owl* in Chelsea, Quebec, in May.
Derek, Tom, Ray, and Sean Dickinson begin a cross-Canada road trip in June.
Tom films small part in the big-screen flick *Superstar* in August.
Tom appears on the *Open Mike with Mike Bullard* late-night talk show and makes the host vomit in November.
MTV buys the rights for *The Tom Green Show* in December.

1999 *The Tom Green Show* debuts on MTV in the United States on January 25.
Tom appears on *Late Night with David Letterman* on February 24.
Tom is made spokesperson for Pepsi One in March.
Tom and his parents appear on *Oprah* on May 7.
Tom signs a development deal with Touchstone Pictures, a division of Walt Disney Co., to write and star in his own movies in August.

2000 Tom returns to Ottawa to film segments for his MTV show.
Tom spoofs local media by holding a "mock" press conference.
Tom appears with former White House intern Monica Lewinsky who launches her line of handbags.